For my mother
and in memory of my father,
my brother Ian and
my sister-in-law Helen

Biographical note

Michael Bayley is an Anglican priest. He was ordained in 1962 to a curacy on a council estate in Leeds. His experience there led him to do a postgraduate course in social administration at Sheffield University to explore the relationship between the community at large, the social services and the church. During that course this interest became focussed on the way in which community care was understood which, in turn, led to five years research and the ground-breaking book Mental Handicap and Community Care (Routledge & Kegan Paul, 1973). He was appointed a lecturer in social administration in 1973 and continued to work on the relationship between the statutory services and the community. His research in Dinnington embraced health and housing as well as social services and was published under the title Local Health and Welfare: Is partnership possible? (with Rosalind Seyd and Alan Tennant). Early retirement from the university gave him the opportunity to undertake the project which led to this book. He is now associate vicar at St Mary's Bramall Lane, an inner city church next to Sheffield United football ground, where he is working with the churches, community groups, local businesses and other members of the community for the social and economic regeneration of the area, a process which includes the social and health services and, of course, people with learning difficulties. He is married with four children and two grandchildren.

Contents

Acknowledgements

I am grateful to the Joseph Rowntree Foundation for their generous and sympathetic support. They gave critical and imaginative encouragement to the changing emphasis of the project, which I believe has enabled me to tackle more fundamental issues than if I had been compelled to stick rigidly to the original research brief. I am grateful in particular to Linda Ward of the Foundation and also to members of my advisory committee - Gina Armstrong, Ann Brechin, Tim Booth, Wendy Booth, Catherine Dobson, Margaret Flynn, Morag McGrath, Mary Myers and Alan Tennant. They were generous with their time and energy and their help and support were invaluable. So also was the help of Richard Parrott who worked with me on thinking through the conceptual framework of the book. His ability to combine imaginative practice with thoughtful reflection did much to help me bring together theory, principle and practice. The degree to which this is successful owes much to him. I am deeply indebted to him and grateful for the time we have spent working together.

I would like to record my particular thanks to Barbara Calligan for permission to use her poem, Michael, and to her husband Michael who passed on that permission to me. Barbara Calligan is unable to speak. The poem was first published in the Newsletter of Calderdale Advocacy, whose co-ordinator, Hilary Dyter, kindly put me in touch with Michael Calligan.

The project was essentially collaborative. I worked with a range of workers from the social services department, the health authority, one particular general practice, the churches, volunteers, people's families and the people with learning difficulties themselves. I am profoundly grateful to them for their generous co-operation. It meant that I was able to draw on a great wealth of knowledge and experience.

Marg Walker reduced the chaos of my writing to an immaculate typescript with accuracy, speed and good humour. Ann Lewin helped me put punctuation in the right places. I am grateful to them both.

Michael Bayley

Preface

The origins of the research for this book go back to 1988 when there was much less talk about the importance of friendship for people with learning difficulties than there is now. The relationships of people with learning difficulties are now taken much more seriously. However, as this book makes clear, we have a long way to go before we can say that our society gives people with learning difficulties adequate opportunities to develop a full range of satisfying relationships. My hope is that this book will help us in that direction and make people more aware of the ways in which such relationships need to be supported.

Much of the book is about the very mundane and ordinary things that need to be done to help people with learning difficulties make their lives more interesting and to enable them to develop relationships. Thus it will be relevant not just for people who make policy but also for those on the front line of care, whether families or paid workers. I am sorry that I have not had the opportunity to expand on ways in which the approach I am advocating is relevant to National Vocational Qualifications. Working in a way that supports the development of relationships should be part of the training, thinking and practice of all those working with people with learning difficulties. This project showed how often this was *not* the case.

Throughout the text I refer to various people to illustrate particular points. Because members of my advisory group said they found it difficult to remember their names, I have listed them in alphabetical order with a thumbnail sketch and page reference to where more details about them can be found (Appendix C). All names have been altered and people's circumstances disguised.

I felt that details about the areas in which the project took place were only of secondary importance but some members of my advisory group felt that some information should be given. I have therefore provided a description of the areas in Appendix D.

Quotations

Unless otherwise identified, the quotations at the start of each chapter come from: Atkinson, D. and Williams, F. (1990) Know Me As I Am: An anthology of prose, poetry and art by people with learning difficulties, London: Hodder & Stoughton.

Chapter I
Introduction

I'm happy with my life because I've got a boyfriend. Without him I'd be miserable.

Friends are important, otherwise you'd be lonely. People are more important than money. (Women's Group: William Brinson, London)

Stan Rivers' story

At first sight Stan Rivers' story may be seen as a success. He is 30, has learning difficulties, poor speech and has been further handicapped by childhood, adolescence and early adulthood spent in care. Stan looks, and feels, noticeably 'different'.

Despite these obstacles, he leads an active and outwardly ordinary life. He lives in an ordinary house in a quiet neighbourhood, belongs to the working men's club where he is well known and liked, and is a member of an ordinary rambling group and cycling group. He is usually out with one or the other at weekends and even takes occasional holidays with them. The residential unit he lived in as a young adult is in the neighbourhood so he knows his locality well. In turn, he himself is well-known. He has important relationships with staff at his day centre.

Stan is self-conscious about being 'different' and has developed coping strategies. Because he dislikes showing his bus pass ("I am mentally handicapped"), he prefers cycling to public transport. Having learned what constitutes an 'under £10 shop' he can use the supermarket and not be embarrassed when asked for more money than the £10 note he has just confidently handed over. He saves and always seems to have more in the bank than me, even though he lives only on benefit. He enjoys music and has a large tape collection. The local video library knows Stan and recommends films, thus avoiding problems arising from being unable to read TV listings.

He receives one weekly visit from a home help (who assists with cleaning and shopping only, company being more important than direct help) and one weekly visit from myself, the social worker, with extra contact if requested.

Stan dresses smartly and gets on with people. But sometimes, having visited him, and without his suggesting any problems or difficulties, I want to cry. His deep sense of loneliness or 'aloneness' is nearly unbearable: no soulmate, close companion or sexual partner, no love. He is confused about his disability, unsure whether it is illness or punishment, supernatural or accident. The media thrusts images of perfect men and women at him and he wants a life to match them. He wants marriage with a beautiful (fantasy) woman, a family (he has been rejected by his own), material success and a car. Stan has less ability than most to separate fantasy and stylised image from reality. By the standards of a TV ad, he judges himself badly. Unable to articulate this in words, he played me sad music or songs of lost romance. He is deeply unhappy.

At one point Stan went into rigid immobile states, like seizures, lasting half an hour or more. These events often occurred at the day centre, often in the company of a key member of staff to whom he felt particularly close. All the many hospital tests he had undergone proved negative. Things started to deteriorate. The situation at the day centre approached crisis, the hospital was frustrated with what appeared to be a series of false alarms and Stan seemed to be heading for a breakdown. This would have been catastrophic since it would have further reinforced his poor self image. My supervisor and I decided it would be worth exploring whether the 'seizures' had emotional origins. Stan and I had a long, intense and moving discussion. He asked questions he had never asked before; I answered as truthfully as I could and the pain was acute. Finally he asked: would he ever get better? He had lived with this question all his life and now knew the answer. My words felt hollow (How could I appreciate his agony?) but we turned to a discussion of his many successes in the face of great difficulties. Afterwards, the seizures stopped but Stan still feels alone. A lifetime's damage to personal esteem and self-confidence cannot be undone quickly. The realities of his life, the images he aspires to all remain and are here to stay.

What this underlined for me is the central importance of the personal and interpersonal world to us all, a lesson particularly relevant in the brave new world of community care. By the criteria of care management, here was a man with a successful 'care package', a stable if not improving situation, progressively lower needs for practical support and formal involvement. Finding the problems meant digging long and hard.

In the language of the formal review, Stan's problems were in the category 'social, spiritual, aesthetic', one where people cough, embarrassed, say 'Doesn't go to church' and move quickly on. Stan is lonely and unhappy, and needs time-consuming, delicate and personal attention. He must understand himself, value himself and be a friend to himself before finding companionship in others. We must work with his heart and feelings, with his social networks, and create new welcoming networks, if he is to feel he can belong.

This graphic painful story from a social worker portrays the central dilemma with which this book struggles. It is the fundamental human question of 'Who am I?' which people with learning difficulties must tackle with fewer resources than most. They are not immune from questions about the meaning and purpose of life and they must face them from a context which makes it difficult to gain a sense of being loved, valued and worthwhile.

Difficult, but certainly not impossible. While it is vital to be aware of Stan's pain, it is equally important not to ignore the profound sense of fulfilment conveyed by 'A Poem to Michael'.

A Poem to Michael
From my heart to you,
I want to say
I love you,
Our wedding means to me,
I didn't believe that would be possible to me.

I want to express
my feelings when you shed tears for me,
Your pain is my pain,
and I feel it deeply,
I worry and think a great deal about it.

From the day of our wedding
I have wanted you to know,
that you are very, very close to my heart,
I want our future to be happy,
to always be together,
and to share everything.

I know how you feel,
how tired you get,
helping me,
washing me,
bathing me,
dressing me,
feeding me,
pushing my wheelchair,
shopping for me,
looking after me.

For me Michael
My life has meaning with you.

From your wife, Barbara

The project around which this book is based addresses the context within which people with learning difficulties live, so that they may approach Barbara's sense of herself rather than Stan's. That wasn't the way I expressed things to start with, but a remorseless logic has pushed me back to more fundamental issues.

The friendship barrier

Concern about the experiences of people leaving hospitals and hostels provided the starting point. Many schemes dealing with this have had considerable success and have impressively widened the opportunities for those involved. Good examples are the Nimrod scheme[1], the Wells Road Service[2], movements from long-stay hospitals into different parts of Somerset[3], the Northumberland scheme whereby severely disabled young people transferred to ordinary housing from Northgate Hospital[4], the Barnardo's scheme in Liverpool for profoundly handicapped children[5], small living units in Wessex researched by Felce and colleagues[6], and the work of Booth, Simons and Booth in the Kirklees Relocation Project[7]. Improvements include better health, physical appearance, mobility and presentation of self, the ability to undertake more tasks, and a richer social life. The organisational detail needed to attain these goals is better understood – for example, not having separate cooking or cleaning staff in residential units, budget autonomy, adequately trained staff and individual programmes regularly reviewed by all concerned including the person with learning difficulties.

The gains are important but all schemes hit the same barrier – integration with the local community is usually superficial.

Felce[8] writes of the small units housing severely and profoundly handicapped adults in Wessex: *Despite high level family and community contact, the range and context of experience (eg. the preponderance of immediate family in their social network and reliance on staff for the majority of community contact) still indicates the need for progress in order to achieve substantial social integration with the mainstream of community life.*

Cattermole et al,[9] examining the lives of people with mild learning difficulties who achieved greater independence, reported: *The most disturbing finding showed that even those active individuals who took part in a variety of more integrative activities failed to get to know non-handicapped people... They were not able to make mutually satisfying friendships with the ordinary people whose company they valued.*

Atkinson and Ward's account of people moving from long-stay hospitals into the community in Somerset[3] is one of the more optimistic. But they write: *The five people (out of 50) who had moved beyond com-*

munity acceptance to the next stage of community participation are exceptions. Most people in the study have settled for far less.

As Firth and Rapley[10] say, even in imaginative community settings, relationships for most people with a learning difficulty are limited to their own family and friends of their family; staff and relatives and friends of staff; household members and their relatives or acquaintances; and professionals.

Firth and Rapley cite the work of Saxby and her colleagues[11], who studied the use of shops, cafes and public houses by adults with severe and profound learning difficulties. They comment: *Despite the fact that increased participation took place in the community, social interactions with the public were of short duration and there appeared to have been very few relationships which could possibly be described as friendship.*

This issue was recognised by the Wells Road Service and two community support workers were appointed to develop 'an ordinary community life' for people in the scheme. Having enjoyed considerable success, the service has been phased out. Linda Ward[12] underlines the problem: *The disturbing lack of close, continuing personal relationships in the lives of people with learning difficulties (outside their family or staff paid to be with them) is only just beginning to be addressed.*

Julie Wilkinson looked at the quality of life enjoyed by residents of the two houses in the Wells Road service. She found their routine had become monotonous and they spent much of their time sitting round the kitchen table drinking cups of tea[13].

Booth, Simons and Booth[14] seem justified in their conclusion that: *Study after study has found that a move into the community results in most people making greater use of community facilities, but few developing social networks that reach out into the wider society. Our research was no exception.*

Flynn's study of 88 people who had moved out of hospitals and hostels includes an eloquent account of how difficult things can be. Apart from acute social isolation many are victimised. A single woman had a particularly difficult time: *One time when I got my money a man followed me and I took a short cut back and he got me against a wall, beat me and took my purse... I don't have many fits now. I do when anything happens that upsets me. Like when I was mugged, and when I've been robbed. I've been robbed three times in two years here. That's why I always keep my curtains closed. This (flat) is all I could get. I'd like to move because of the kids. They throw eggs and all sorts at my windows. They call me names and throw things at me when I'm out. The window cleaner can't get the mess off the windows. The police can't do anything. No one can stop them. My brother always walks me back if I go out...*

Flynn brings out the importance of this: *Absence of victimisation is important... people who experience victimisation are unable to trust others and, regarding themselves as prey, they do not or cannot take the necessary steps to form relationships. Some people are too frightened to leave their homes, and inevitably this reduces their opportunities to meet others.*[15]

All this indicates that there are varying barriers to full and satisfying integration into the community which only a few people with learning difficulties manage to pass.

A community development approach

How can these barriers be addressed? Richardson and Ritchie recognise the need for an effective community response: *While we suspect that most schemes concerned with social skills are aimed at the mentally handicapped person, some attention should be given to schemes concerned with the ways in which other people, particularly non-handicapped, respond.*[16]

A serious defect in community care strategy is its failure to recognise that work is needed to enable people and organisations in the community to respond adequately to those with learning difficulties.

A number of issues deserve attention:

(1) Focusing on a limited geographical area. Understanding how organisations in the area work, enabling them to build appropriate and durable links with people with learning difficulties and with other organisations. Looking for mutually complementary needs in the area (eg. an old person who would like to be visited and a person with learning difficulties who would like to visit). Establishing the overall social and political context within which the project is operating (eg. one residents

association said too many people with special needs were being placed in the area).

(2) Recognising that geographical limitations need not always be strictly applied. Potentially important links may exist outside.

(3) Finding how professionals and service agencies may fit into and support the process while not taking it over or disrupting it.

(4) Concentrating on the process through which friendships are encouraged to ensure people with learning difficulties gain maximum control over their lives, including possibilities for corporate action.

(5) Being alert to the range of bodies, groups, organisations, services, etc. that need to be considered.

Although this aspect of the community development approach is important it was not the most significant influence on the project. The real danger was that the project might have turned into little more than the traditional service delivery model plus a few volunteers and links with local organisations. While this has real value, and indeed was adopted, it does not amount to a full-blooded community development approach for which the fundamental tenet is to take time to understand the culture, the assumptions and the priorities of those who need help. The strong anthropological element to the work has been expressed well by Ramcharan and Grant: *The researcher will, like the anthropologist, have to become immersed in the field in order to discover the subject's meaningful world and their systems of rationality.*[17]

In practice, this means uncovering past and existing networks of friendships and acquaintances, sorting out the services and organisations within which people with learning difficulties, their families and those associated with them, live and have lived, and understanding their values, assumptions, strengths, weaknesses and ways of operating. In effect, it means establishing a broad social history of the person concerned and understanding the meaning of various aspects of their life to the people with learning difficulties. This becomes progressively more important. An example from Boga, a district in north-west Zaire in West Africa, illustrates the need to think radically 'to discover the subject's meaningful world and their system of rationality'.

It was not until a child died of malnutrition that health workers began to question what was wrong with the health services. Until then, they had considered their primary health care programme to be very success- ful. When they began talking to local people about health, they real- ised that the western understanding of health was failing to meet the needs of the community. The child who had died had died of 'misery'. His mother knew that this could not be cured at the church hospital.

The project workers realised that they had to gain a proper under- standing of the local people's concept of health: *In the course of the discussions, the word 'obusinge' was repeated frequently. 'Obusinge' is a Kihema word which means 'health' but it means much more than the western concept of health. 'Obusinge' was a sense of health, well- being and peace, on the one hand, and a sense of hope and optimism on the other. The sense of hope came not only from God but also from the strength of family and community relationships.*

Discussions revealed that these conditions did not relate to the indi- vidual but to the family as a unit. It was the human relationships within the family and the community which created the sense of well-being associated with 'obusinge'. For example, a person living alone could not achieve 'obusinge' even if he or she had wealth and health. On the other hand, an old person living in the comfort of his family could die in a state of 'obusinge'. It was therefore decided that 'obusinge' should be defined in terms of conditions of family life.[18]

Having understood how the villagers defined health, workers were able to develop the project with them on the basis of the more holistic no- tion of health that the villagers held. Previously the project had not fully connected with local reality.

Development of understanding

Discovering the meaning of various aspects of the lives of those with learning difficulties with whom I was working was a gradual process. The initial emphasis was on integration, primarily through the develop- ment of friendships (ie. overcoming the 'friendship barrier' mentioned above). In trying to discover people's interests and then linking those people with others of like mind, I realised the main focus was no longer on integration but on friendship.

In an early paper I wrote: *The central importance of* friendship *is the core of the work which is described here.*

Initially the plan was to contact a very limited number of people, only 12, who were living by themselves or with a partner, to discover their social links and find ways of extending them. This proved to be too limited and did not take account adequately of the network of contacts and the complex interaction in the area as a whole. Appreciating the importance of local links led to two changes in the population included in the project. First, people living with their families were included. They can suffer isolation just as anyone discharged from hospital or hostel can. Second, people living in hostels in the area were included. Both groups were actually or potentially part of the local networks of friends. Excluding them would have denied the very community development principles on which the project was founded.

It became apparent that I needed a wide range of contacts. With the help of the local Case Register, I contacted just over 50 people with learning difficulties. They included people living on their own, with a partner, with parents and in hostels, and varied from those with quite profound difficulties who were unable to speak, to those who managed their lives with a competence many would envy.

As a consequence it became clear there was a need for a broad spectrum of relationships (ie, the focus moved from integration, to friendships and sharing interests, to the need for a range of contacts, to the need for a range of relationships). It was not sufficient to focus only on friendships. Friendships are formed and carried on within the context of a network of relationships.

The feeling that one is valued and that one is making a contribution to the lives of others, can only be gained through personal relationships. Relationships of all kinds help define who we are... Without relationships we cannot know what we are like, or what kind of person we would like to be.[19]

If I wanted to address how to give people a sense of self-esteem and being valued, I had to identify the full range of relationships needed. This goes way beyond identifying common interests from which friendships might form. Indeed, one reason I looked more carefully at the range of relationships was because some links were breaking down or not even starting for reasons I did not understand fully.

Focus on integration

An early project discussion paper explained: *The centre of the research is real integration into the community and looking at both the processes and how integration affects quality of life... As far as possible the research needs to concentrate on features of our society and the localities in which people live which encourage or discourage, help or hinder integration and the particular strategies in the community which work because this is where both practice and research are almost totally lacking.*[20]

The initial plan concentrated on only 12 people with learning difficulties; intensive work involved no more than three at a time. The first hiccup was the length of time it took for the social services department to allow me to approach people who were its clients. Permission to become involved with two men, Philip Brindley and Jason Havering, living in a house owned and run by the health authority took only a matter of days. The men had lived in the house for nearly five years and managers were concerned about their minimal links with the area, even though they used many facilities.

Five months later, having eventually obtained social services department permission, I started work with a group of people with learning difficulties who met with two specialist social workers weekly at Oldale Community Centre. Most had previously lived in the nearby hostel and had moved out into their own accommodation. The workers thought that some had reached the stage of wanting to establish better outside links and thus would be ideal. I worked primarily with a married couple, a couple living together and an older single man living alone. However, this work took place within the context of the relationships with other members of the group whom I also got to know.

Focus on interests

While I was working primarily with Philip Brindley and Jason Havering and the group that met at Oldale Community Centre, I concentrated on trying to discover activities, interests, skills and enthusiasms – anything which really lit up an individual. The thinking was that if two people shared an activity which they enjoyed, the chances of a friendship developing were quite good, far greater than if a volunteer visited out of a sense of goodwill but with no obvious common ground.

This seemed a most attractive route. Edward Pilkington writes of the Leisure Link scheme in Cheshire: *Leisure Link aims to give people with learning difficulties the chance to interact in exactly the same way as everyone else – through developing interests and sharing them*

*with others. In this scheme volunteers are replaced by 'leisure sharers':
people willing to team up with a disabled person in the pursuit of a
common passion.*[21]

Wider range of contacts needed

However, when I focused primarily on shared interests the results were
limited and took a disproportionate amount of time and effort. It was
something of a consolation to read that Leisure Link had found the
way 'steep and thorny... while 57 people were referred to the project
in its first year, only 16 potential leisure sharers came forward. Moreo-
ver, of the 16 links that were made, only half took root and became
established'. Part of my problem lay in the small numbers of people I
worked with. I found I spent time waiting for people to respond: for a
Gilbert and Sullivan Society to decide whether they would be happy
for a person with learning difficulties to attend rehearsals, for the minister of the local Methodist church to remember to ask the Scout Mas-
ter if the scouts would be prepared to take someone swimming (I never
got a reply to that one). Waiting was an integral part of the approach;
people can be encouraged, but ultimately they make their own decision and this takes time. I realised it would be positively helpful if I had
more requests out because it would be easier to timetable the inevitable delays without the whole project being held up.

I also found that looking for a range of contacts rather than just one is
more productive because it turns up other possibilities; choice and
sensitive matching require as many people as possible on both sides
of the equation; and a wide range of people offers a potentially wide
range of contacts and relationships, as already mentioned.

Before I could work with more people I had to find them. The area has
a case register of all people known to have learning difficulties and
those in charge agreed to help me. They wrote to people asking if they
would be prepared to meet me and the names of those that agreed
were passed to me. Usually I visited the people themselves and spoke
to their parents or carers, staff at the day care units or residential units
they attended or lived in. I was usually able to talk to their key worker.
I also contacted adult education staff where relevant.

This proved invaluable. The range of people and situations I found
provided the essential data which led to the development in thinking
already described. At this stage, my role was becoming more of a

broker, varying from little more than making an introduction to heavy involvement in helping someone develop contacts. It is the source of many of the illustrations which follow.

An inadequate theoretical framework

I have sketched what happened during the life of this project from two perspectives: the development of my thinking and the development of the action. Let me add a third perspective: how this relates to previous work in the field.

Three books were particularly influential:

Ties and Connections: An ordinary community life for people with learning difficulties, produced by the King's Fund[22]; Developing Friendships: Enabling people with learning difficulties to make and maintain friends, by Ann Richardson and Jane Ritchie[23], and From Acquaintance to Friendship, by Hugh Firth and Mark Rapley[10]. All three, and especially Firth and Rapley who drew on the insights of the earlier two, gave many practical suggestions about how to proceed. The notion of friendship coming via acquaintance draws on Firth and Rapley, as does the emphasis on finding shared interests and seeking ways into local organisations. In my proposal to the Joseph Rowntree Foundation I described Firth and Rapley's book as a major resource. Later chapters show how I think they hit a number of nails on the head. One example, in Ties and Connections, picked up the need for a range of friendships: 'The need for a partner has to be understood in the context of a wider need for a range of satisfying friendships'.[24] I also endorse fully their emphasis on maintaining existing relationships.

But gradually I became aware I was working with an inadequate theoretical framework. I had expected the project would be frustrating since friendships do not lend themselves to easy manipulation. However, I had not expected to achieve so little after spending so much effort for so long. Failures made me look more searchingly at the theoretical model I was using. It is ironic and instructive that a project designed to be practical forced a re-examination of background theory – the subject of the next chapter.

Firth and Rapley wrote: *Some of those who were asked to comment on drafts of this book hoped we could describe the results of our approach in practice. Does it work?, they asked. We do not yet know.*[25]

My answer is 'sometimes' and I hope to throw more light on why it works on some occasions and not on others.

A further perspective

There is one other perspective. The original proposal laid down a clear programme of work and was initiated by putting certain ideas into practice. There was nothing mechanical about this and I always knew I had a great deal to learn.

What started as a project run by me turned into a venture shared with others. When I explained that I wanted to explore and develop people's friendships, I received a warm response. Few were able to produce answers but many supplied invaluable insights and contributions. I wasn't happy about all the practices I encountered but I also saw some first rate and very imaginative work. It seemed that existing good practice had been inadequately acknowledged. The work I did myself – presented here – has been enriched immeasurably by the experience and insights of people working in this field. The material I used extends beyond the people I saw and draws on this wider experience. Obviously I am responsible for what I have written, but the thoughts, wisdom and experience of a much wider group of people are also reflected.

While practitioners' experience has been important, it is that of people with learning difficulties which has bitten most fiercely into my consciousness. Above all else I hope what I have written does justice to that experience.

References

1. One of many relevant reports: Evans, G., Todd, S., Blunden, R., Porterfield, J. and Ager, A. (1987) A New Style of Life: The Impact of Moving into an Ordinary House on the Lives of People with a Mental Handicap, Mental Handicap in Wales Applied Research Unit, Research Report No. 17.
2. Ward, L. (1988) Whose Home is it Anyway?, Community Care, 14 January; Thwarting Ordinary Lives, Community Care, 21 January.
3. Atkinson, D. and Ward, L. (1987), Relationships and Opportunities in the Community for People with a Mental Handicap, Re-assessing Community Care (ed. Malin, N.), London: Croom Helm.
4. Shearer, A. (1986) Building Community, London: Campaign for People with Mental Handicaps/King's Fund, pp.119-126.
5. Alaszewski, A. and Bie Nio Ong (1987) Community Care for Profoundly Mentally Handicapped Children, Re-assessing Community Care (ed. Malin, N.), London: Croom Helm.
6. In particular, Felce, D. and Toogood, S. (1986) Close to Home: a housing service and its impact on the lives of nine profoundly and severely mentally handicapped adults, Kidderminster: BIMH Publications.
7. Booth, T., Simons, K. and Booth, W. (1990) Outward Bound: Relocation and Community Care for People with Learning Diffciulties, Milton Keynes: Open University Press.

8. Felce, D. (1986) Housing for severely and profoundly handicapped adults, Eisenberg, N. and Glasgow, D. (eds) Current Issues in Clinical Psychology, Aldershot: Gower.

9. Cattermole, M., Jahoda, A. and Markova, I. (1987) Training for Independent Living in Mental Handicap Hospitals and Adult Training Centres: Final Report to Scottish Home and Health Department, Department of Psychology, University of Stirling.

10. Firth, H. and Rapley, M.T.J. (1990) From Acquaintance to Friendship: Issues for People with Learning Disabilities, Kidderminster: BIMH Publications, p.30.

11. Saxby, H., Thomas, M., Felce, D. and de Kock, U. (1985) The Use of Shops, Cafes and Public Houses by Severely and Profoundly Mentally Handicapped Adults, Health Care Evaluation Research Team, University of Southampton.

12. Ward, L. (1988) Thwarting Ordinary Lives, *Community Care*, 21 January, p.23.

13. Wilkinson, J. Personal communication.

14. Ref. 7, p.180.

15. Flynn, M. (1989) Independent Lives for Adults with Mental Handicap: A Place of their Own, London: Cassell, p.65 and p.118.

16. Richardson, A. and Ritchie, J. (1987) Social Support for People with a Mental Handicap: some preliminary considerations, p.11.

17. Ramcharan, P. and Grant, G. (1992) Empowering Persons with a Disadvantage within the Research Process, Paper presented at 9th IASSMD World Congress, p.4.

18. Contact (Christian Medical Commission, Geneva) No. 128, December 1992, pp.i & 5.

19. Ref. 10, p.19.

20. Bayley, M.J. (1990) Directions and Priorities, Unpublished discussion paper.

21. Pilkington, E. (1991) Pastime with good company, Search, 10 August 1991, pp.12-14.

22. Ties and Connections: An ordinary community life for people with learning difficulties (1988) London: King's Fund Centre.

23. Richardson, A. and Ritchie, J. (1989) Developing Friendships: Enabling people with learning difficulties to make and maintain friends, London: Policy Studies Institute in association with Social and Community Planning Research.

24. Ref. 22, p.29.

25. Ref. 10, p.171.

Chapter II
The range of relationships

I love my mum and dad very much because they are my family. They love me too because they had me as a baby. (Susan Bunsall: William Brinson Centre, London).

Most of my friends I've had for 20 years and they've become part of my life. We've been through life together and have got common points of interest. Sometimes you make new friends, when your friends from school move away to get married. (Terry).

As I've got older, I've got few friends and lots of acquaintances. A friend is someone who knows all about you and loves you just the same: A friend to me is someone really special. (Margaret) ('A Chance to Speak' class: City Lit, London).

In Chapter I, I argued that we need relationships to gain a sense of being loved and valued, a sense of self-esteem and meaning in our lives and to become fulfilled. This chapter explores what that range of relationships should cover.

Relationships are not transferable. They must also be various to meet ourdifferent needs. The Open University's course Patterns for Living provides a good starting point in defining basic needs:

> The question of what people get from relationships with other people was considered at a conference of people with mental handicap, parents and residential workers in America. The quotes below are from the report of that conference (Personal Relationships for Persons with Development Disabilities, 1985).
>
> **Knowing who we are.** It is through our relationships with others that we learn about ourselves and also, at least partly, become the people we are. 'A person gains confidence as he or she is successful at getting along with others he or she likes'.
>
> **Affection and security.** Others give us love and emo-

tional security, but they also give us the possibility of loving and feeling needed. 'It's almost as if relationships is a life safety issue'.

Sharing feelings and ideas. We can confide in others and they in us. Close relationships can offer understanding and possibilities for talking about intimate feelings. 'Don't live on lonely street'.

Activities and interests. Personal relationships offer our main social activities, such as companionship, conversation, leisure, play and common interests. 'Put simply, having friends is fun'.

Practical help. This refers to all kinds of material and active support people offer each other, including lending money, baby-sitting, pushing the car and so on. 'Most people get practical help from others who are nearby'.

Advice and information. Other people are a main source of information and advice. 'People learn from each other'.[1]

This matches the typology proposed by Weiss and taken up by Bulmer in his book, The Social Basis of Community Care. Weiss, researching lone parents, found relationships were differentiated and one was not an adequate substitute for another: *In the absence of membership in a social network which shared their central life concerns, individuals experience severe distress.*[2]

Bulmer points out how Weiss shows:
The provisions of marriage could not be supplied by friendship... nor could the provisions of friendship be supplied by marriage... Weiss was led to conclude that individuals have requirements for well-being that can only be met through relationships. But different relational provisions depend upon different, usually incompatible, relational assumptions. Thus a relationship with a friend, a child or a spouse all rest on different bases, and a degree of specialisation occurs in what is provided by a particular relationship.[3]

The strength of Weiss' typology is that he gets below the social roles people play and addresses the different emotional and cognitive needs. I quote Bulmer's summary of Weiss' six types:

(1) *Attachment and intimacy* is provided in relationships from which individuals gain a sense of security and place. Feelings can be expressed freely and without self-consciousness, and in such relationships individuals feel comfortable and at home. The absence of such relationships is likely to lead to loneliness and restlessness. Attachment is provided by marriage or other sustained sexual partnership, in some close relationships between a woman and a close friend, sister or mother; and for some men in relationships with 'buddies'.

(2) *Social integration* is provided by relationships in which participants share concerns because they are in the same situation or striving for similar objectives, and can exchange experience, information and ideas. This may be provided by friends or work colleagues. In the area of social support, self-help groups may often provide a means for the social integration of the otherwise isolated person.

(3) Opportunities for *nurturance*, (ie. giving nurture) where an adult takes responsibility for a child, encourages the development of a sense of being needed, and may also provide a model for care in the future (eg. by a daughter or son of an elderly parent).

(4) *Reassurance of worth* is provided by relationships that demonstrate an individual's competence in some role. This may be provided by work or, for men, by the ability to support and defend a family. The loss of a source of such reassurance is likely to result in decreased self-esteem as with unemployed heads of families.

(5) *Reliable assistance* through the provision of services or resources. Friends and/or neighbours may be a source at some period and in some circumstances, but it is only among close kin that continued assistance may be expected regardless of affective ties. This pattern is evident in patterns of informal support for the elderly. Absence of a relationship offering such assistance is likely to be reflected in increased anxiety and vulnerability.

(6) *Obtaining guidance* is derived from relationships with

respected others, such as priests, doctors, nurses, social workers and counsellors and, on occasion, impersonal advice services which do not involve face-to-face contact.

The only significant difference between that list and the one quoted from the Patterns for Living course is the category of 'nurturance' (the opportunity to give care). However, a 'Five-point guide to relationships' in the Patterns for Living course, lists: (1) Feeling safe with. (2) Feeling good with. (3) Learning from. (4) Benefiting from. (5) Giving to...[4]

Few would argue that in a network of relationships we need to be able to give as well as receive. In other words, to express the vital principle of reciprocity, designated as nurturance by Weiss.

With his five accomplishments: Community Participation, Community Presence, Choices/Rights, Respect and Competence, John O'Brien takes a different approach.[5] Though not strictly comparable, one of the accomplishments points to an omission in Weiss' typology – opportunity for choice – although this may be implicit in the six existing categories. Lack of choice, lack of an opportunity to make decisions, is so much part of the lives of people with learning difficulties that exercise of choice must be included in the range of what relationships need to provide.

This last point is important. Clearly *attachment and intimacy* or *reassurance of worth* are not relationships but are basic needs which relationships can meet. However, it would be pedantic to refer all the time to 'the range of what relationships need to provide' so I will simply refer to 'the range of relationships'. This is discussed further at the beginning of Chapter III.

Weiss' first category, *attachment and intimacy*, needs further consideration. In Figure 1 (p33) I have changed it to *belonging and attachment*. I added *belonging* because it expresses emotional content more powerfully than *attachment* alone. I dropped *intimacy* which my advisory group thought I should reinstate. In part I agree. A real sense of belonging and attachment will generally be expressed through an intimate relationship but it is important to remember that such relationships have long been denied to people with learning difficulties. Intimacy is usually taken for granted but, while often integral, it is not essential: anyone, not just those with learning difficulties, may gain a

sense of belonging and attachment without the relationship being intimate. It seemed important not to be prescriptive about the way a sense
of *belonging and attachment* is gained. Also, intimacy is more a means
than an end: one may be intimate with someone without necessarily
arriving at a sense of belonging and attachment.

Relationship vacuums

The above seven categories of relationship are not a selection from
which one or two may be chosen: they represent, albeit inadequately,
fundamental elements necessary for our social, psychological and
spiritual health. This is especially the case with *attachment*. The Patterns of Living[6] course refers to relationship vacancies, a useful concept, but I prefer vacuum. A vacuum is likely to be filled up. It will suck
in from outside, precisely what appears to happen in many instances.

*Weiss argues that the relationship that provides attachment is of cen-
tral importance in the organisation of one's life. Individuals will tend to
organise their lives around those relationships which provide them with
attachment – usually a spouse or partner – but it could be a grown
child or a close friend. Other relationships are then integrated with this
central relationship. Lack of intimate relationships may have distressing consequences.*[7]

Stan Rivers is someone whose life lacked that central relationship of
attachment. Mark Hastings is another.

Mark Hastings, in his middle twenties, lived with his elderly widowed
mother in a comfortable, owner-occupied, semi. His apparently normal social competence suggested he should be able to read and recognise numbers, but he could do neither. Mark's mother suffered from
a bad back and needed his help with household tasks, like making the
bed and carrying the shopping, which he did without any trouble. But
Mark's life was restricted. He sometimes went out on his own, loved
watching the bowls in the local park, but always stayed on the edge.
His relationship with his mother was tense; he resented her trying to
organise his life. When he could not cope – for example, when made
to feel foolish because he could not read – he exploded. Recently, his
violence had become only verbal and might be expressed by march-
ing dramatically out of the room, but it was enough to prevent him
forming relationships.

At one stage I thought I had made some progress in enabling Mark to widen his social circle. A rambling club proved welcoming and understanding. Mark was able to go on his own and became involved in mid-week activities as well as weekend walks. His social life became far richer and he met a wide cross-section of people who were disposed to be friendly. Occasional setbacks made him feel slighted but club members were resilient and it seemed Mark was becoming accepted and valued.

One friendly and welcoming member was an attractive young woman, a bit younger than Mark. She smiled at him but her behaviour indicated no more than friendliness. She was going out with another member, though they were not (then) engaged. Mark saw her smile as a signal that she wanted the romantic involvement for which he was longing. It fell to me to take a long walk with Mark and tell him his romantic overtures were unwelcome and that she was already 'committed'. It was also necessary, and even more painful, to discuss with Mark how his disabilities would affect his relationships, especially intimate ones (an issue I will return to later).

Lack of a close relationship that gave a sense of attachment and belonging caused Mark to feel loss and to behave inappropriately in a different category of relationship. Relationships within the club could probably be described as 'social integration'; behaviour appropriate in an intimate relationship is inappropriate in a social setting like a church or club. It is of course possible to progress from a friendly relationship in a social setting to a more intimate one but, for someone like Mark, who has a relationship vacuum, especially at the level of 'belonging and attachment', there is always a danger that other relationships at the 'social integration' level will be inappropriately used and consequently break down.

All too often, people in Mark's situation have been excluded from learning the almost imperceptible signals which govern social behaviour. Thus intellectual disability is exacerbated by lack of social experience.

Fundamentally, where someone has a vacuum in her or his range of relationships, especially at the 'belonging and attachment' level, other relationships may be sucked into that vacuum. The result is inappropriate social behaviour. Despite everyone's best efforts, Mark left the club with a deep sense of rejection.

What type of relationships will give Mark a sense of self-worth? He confronted one of the most painful situations for people with learning difficulties: the desire to have a romantic relationship with someone who did not have learning difficulties. What advice do you give? Try to meet someone of your level of ability who may reciprocate your desire? Keep trying and keep being disappointed like other people? But other people do not start with the odds stacked against them in quite the same way. How can Mark be enabled to accept his limitations and capitalise on his abilities, especially when he is living with a parent who needs those abilities and who undermines his confidence?

Arthur Needles was in his mid-thirties and lived with his parents. He could read quite well and write a bit, but was unsure of himself socially and lacked the confidence to walk around the streets alone. They were an isolated family and seldom went out. Arthur spent the day watching television and driving his mother frantic by digging holes in the settee with his fingers. He was keen to develop his reading but there were no vacancies in adult education classes in the area. A retired teacher offered her services and we arranged for them to meet weekly for an hour or so for a literacy class in a community centre. This proved very successful. Arthur described Jennifer Parsons, the teacher, as 'ace' and obviously felt he had made a friend. Jennifer was delighted with Arthur's rapid progress and with the good relationship they had established. Her reservation was significant: "I don't want him to become too fond of me. I don't want him to depend on me."

Arthur's situation was not so critical or extreme as Mark's but there was still a danger of Jennifer being sucked into a more intimate and demanding role than she was able to offer because of a gaping hole in Arthur's life for a close relationship with a woman. Things were eased slightly by another younger woman who took Arthur to a good basic education class for adults so that not all of Arthur's hunger for friendship fell on Jennifer. However, the issue was the same – the risk of an inappropriate use of a relationship because of 'relationship vacuums'.

This great hole in the relationships of many people with learning difficulties was picked up by Margaret Flynn in her study of 88 people who had moved into their own homes from hostels or hospitals: *According to social workers, four people had no contact with friends and eleven only had intermittent contact. In the interviews 18 people did not mention contact with others. As a recipient of two marriage invitations and many requests for further contact with the people I met, I have to conclude that some people's networks are wanting.*[8]

This illustrates clearly not just the vacuum in relationships but also the inappropriate use of other categories of relationship.

In both my examples and Margaret Flynn's, the most acutely felt vacuum is in 'belonging and attachment'. The same process operates with other levels of relationships. Jack and Eileen Parsons had been married for five years. Jack had no friends, one reason being that he got very angry when, for example, he was beaten at snooker. His relationship with Eileen, described by the social worker as obsessive, was not a substitute for the weaker ties of ordinary friendship (ie. in the 'social integration' and 'reassurance of worth' categories). Jack needed friends for snooker and similar activities, a need Eileen could not meet.

I started attending the group meeting at Oldale Community Centre just before Christmas and found myself classed as a friend who qualified for a Christmas card from most of the people there. This indicated a vacuum in 'reassurance of worth'; to receive cards confirms you are a person with whom people like to be friends. Atkinson and Williams put the point well: *The absence of friends can lead to an extended definition of friendship. This means, for example, coming to regard neighbours as 'friends' on the flimsy basis of an occasional nod, smile, or kind word... The extended definition of friendship does not remove the feeling of loneliness – but it may disguise the isolation.*[9]

Atkinson and Williams also mention social workers, home helps and other staff who come to be seen as friends. Other factors are at play here but it indicates the need for a full range of relationships to fill the vacuum experienced by many people with learning difficulties and to counteract the tendency to make inappropriate transfers from one category or level of relationship to another. Here the transfer was from 'reliable assistance' or 'obtaining guidance' to 'reassurance of worth' or even 'belonging and attachment'.

To sum up, a full range of relationships, on the lines set out by Weiss, is a common human need. If one level or category is missing, the person will suffer, as with Stan Rivers. Some people with learning difficulties, lacking social skills and/or experience, may make inappropriate transfers, especially from the 'social integration' level to the 'belonging and attachment' level. This is likely to foul up relationships, as it did with Mark Hastings.

Some people appear content without any obvious intimate relationships although there are usually compensatory relationships elsewhere. A clear example comes from the work of Dorothy Atkinson:

Alan Perkins is 50 years old. He lived in a mental handicap hospital for 31 years, then in a group home for two years. Now he lives in a flat in a small block of modern council flats.

He lives alone and has to seek social engagements outside the house. He abandoned not only his group home, but the rest of the mental handicap trappings, the ATC, and other mentally handicapped people. Of the latter, his social worker commented, "I've noticed, out in the street, that if anyone comes along who is handicapped, he will not tolerate them, he puts them down. He's trying to make contact with ordinary people. He doesn't want handicapped people".

Alan seeks to engage neighbours, tradesmen and people in the street. His relations with his neighbours began badly when his electrical tinkerings, in the first weekend, led to the whole block of flats being plunged into darkness, and all televisions silenced. His social worker had to intervene, to remonstrate with Alan, found hiding, and to soothe neighbours' frayed nerves. He has erased this inauspicious start from the communal memory by his subsequent friendliness. He calls on people to chat, and to check that elderly neighbours are well, and they reciprocate with kindness. The neighbours have donated furniture and hung curtains, and now Alan can leave his rent with neighbours when the rent man is due to call. His social worker commented, "They have taken him into their hearts!"

Alan has also expended energy in cultivating tradespeople. The social worker described this investment: "He is aware that people give drinks at Christmas. He likes to make sure he has plenty of drinks in. Then he invites people in, for example the butcher and the greengrocer. I heard them say, 'We'll be round for our drinks Alan', and he replied 'OK, whenever you like' ". Alan engages people out and about in the neighbourhood too, always having time to stop and chat, his social worker observing: "A lot of people know him. A lot of people stop and talk to him". His social worker observed that he has devised a 'strategy of coping', an easy and informal manner, and a genuine interest in others, which is reciprocated, and which has led to the construction of his good supporting network.[10]

It is interesting and disturbing that Alan rejects anyone who is handicapped. Mark and Arthur reacted in a similar way. This issue is considered later.

But another way of coping is by withdrawal: a clear example, Christopher Johnson, raises the vital question of structures. Relationships are sustained and supported by structures – they cannot exist in a vacuum

Relationships and structures

Christopher Johnson brought home the message that relationships and structures must be considered together. He was severely handicapped, unable to speak, hardly responding to anything said to him. When I first visited the house and talked to his widowed mother he lay on the floor and played with his sock. It was hard to see how anything could be done to enrich his life.

His key worker at the day centre he attended (sporadically) mentioned that Mary Cartwright got responses out of Christopher. Who was she? A psychologist, a senior day care worker, or a communication therapist? None of these, in fact, but a severely handicapped woman with little speech, a great sense of fun and inexhaustible energy.

Sadly, Mary had been moved to another day centre about two years previously. Christopher's relationship with her was by far his most positive. Could it be re-established? Could Mary be moved back? No, she was well established in her new centre. Could Christopher be taken at least once a week to the centre she attended? It was quite close to his home. No, the transport and escort needed were not available and there was no prospect of this changing. (It took three weeks to find that out). Could they meet somewhere? Mary had Wednesdays at her hostel – a good day for her to see Christopher. On the first occasion Christopher was ill and the meeting was cancelled. I was booked for the next three Wednesdays, but eventually the day came. The message had not been passed on; a member of staff had taken Mary out and was not expected back for an hour or so! We were unable to try again for six weeks but eventually they met. Mary was certainly pleased to see Christopher. His reactions were difficult to gauge but he certainly did not object. However, after she made him a cup of tea and he drank it, there was nothing they could do together and the visit seemed flat.

Was that the end of the road? If Christopher's key worker was right,

Mary meant more to Christopher than anyone else (except his mother), and she had known him for a good many years. The lead had to be pursued, especially since Christopher was severely handicapped and had to make the most of any relationships he had.

I spent some time with Mary and her key worker to discover Mary's interests. She loved going shopping, going to the park, seeing animals. She responded positively to almost anything. The plan was to allow Christopher to accompany Mary and share her enthusiasm. But for this to happen they needed to meet regularly and that could not depend on me.

In discussions with Mrs Johnson it emerged she had another son who lived nearby, had a car and should be able to take Christopher and herself. After many phone calls a visit took place and seemed to be enjoyed by all parties – Christopher, his mother and his sister-in-law. I left it with Mrs Johnson to fix the next visit and primed the hostel staff. I suggested that next time Christopher might see something new with Mary. Nothing came of it, despite much encouragement, and eventually I gave up. The hostel was short-staffed and the visit was not seen as part of the work. Mrs Johnson was probably too worn down by the daily slog of looking after Christopher.

Apathy or, more accurately, my exhaustion, won the day and Christopher's social life collapsed back into that provided by his mother alone. The structure to support wider social contacts was simply not there. Widening the range of Christopher's relationships meant attending to the structure of his life.

What are the relevant structures?
I say 'structure' to emphasise that we must pay attention to the overall structure of the lives of people with learning difficulties. It may may seem too elaborate a word to describe Christopher Johnson's home or an adult training centre, but these settings make up the structure of his life. Our lives consist of our activities or our presence in different settings. I could say 'the settings which make up the structure' but structure is simpler shorthand.

Experiences during the project suggested that the relevant structures are straightforward. The main ones are: residence/home; work/education/occupation; leisure/social/spiritual; and supportive services and people.

Residence/home

The place where people live has a considerable impact on their relationships. Christopher's situation differed from that of someone living by themselves or with a partner, in a small group home or a hostel. It is vital also to consider where people lived in the past. The significance of such hostels and hospitals will become apparent. The addition of 'home' emphasises that everyone lived somewhere but not everyone had a home.

Work/education/occupation

These experiences are grouped because they are what people do in work time even if they do not work. Only one of the people I saw was in an ordinary job. About half spent at least some time in day care at an adult training centre, or its new manifestation, a local training centre, where there was more emphasis on finding activities in the locality such as helping in or attending a lunch club or going to a local pub. Others combined attendance at day care, provided by the social services department, with adult education classes. Some just attended the latter. Some had no day time occupation. Indeed, one of the strongest impressions was how many people with learning difficulties spent their day wasting time. Many lacked, almost totally, meaningful occupation, often including time they spent in day care. As with residence, past attendance at day or similar centres is also important in understanding present relationships.

Leisure/social/spiritual

This is a much wider category. It links with the previous ones because much day care centre attendance is occupied with leisure activities. However, it is important to know how people occupy themselves outside the nine-to-five period. It can include attendance at the Gateway Club, the PHAB (Physically Handicapped Able Bodied) Club, youth clubs, etc. and also covers spectating at football matches, playing football, going swimming or going to the pub. Matters of the spirit, typically membership of a church, also fall into this category. Flynn and Hirst point out how important this category can be: *When access to paid employment is limited, personal relationships, social contacts and leisure assume a much greater importance, not least in providing activity, variety, a sense of identity and self esteem.*[11]

Supportive services and people

All services from whatever source, apart from residential and day care, come under this heading. In practice they consisted almost entirely of statutory services (mostly health and social services). Also included is support from social workers, community nurses and other community support workers and home helps. Some key workers in day care stray across this boundary by supporting people in their homes.

Parents or other family members sometimes provided important support for those who had moved into their homes. Occasionally, support came purely out of goodwill from unrelated people.

Relating structures to the range of relationships

Structures cannot be considered alone. Those set up with and around Stan Rivers appeared exemplary but left him feeling a great hole inside. Nor should relationships be considered alone because without the structure to support them they will not survive. Only by relating one to the other is it possible to consider key issues such as which structures encourage trusting, intimate relationships, or integration, or self-esteem, or exercise of choice.

Sustaining and developing

However, relationships and structures also need sustaining and developing. Relationships do not develop mechanistically. Getting the structures right is important in enabling relationships to develop, but this is not the end of the matter. Structures only provide the setting which facilitates development of relationships.

A pattern of service which gives priority and importance to sustaining, nurturing and developing the relationships of people with learning difficulties, must accept that this requires commitment of time, energy and resources. People with learning difficulties often continue to need help with their relationships, as do some in the general population. However, with so little normal social experience from which to learn, they have particular needs. They are doubly handicapped.

Many people with learning difficulties find difficulty in transferring their understanding of one situation to a similar but different one. One quite able young man made beans on toast by toasting bread, buttering it, then putting beans on top after opening a tin and heating the contents. Faced with putting creamed mushrooms (from a tin) on toast, he was completely thrown and put the mushrooms on the bread under the grill before toasting the bread. It should never be assumed that people with learning difficulties can make transfers of knowledge automatically and underlines the need for sustaining.

Exchange

Reciprocity is at the heart of all relationships of any emotional depth. This can be a problem for people with learning difficulties who, on the face of it, may have little to give. Bulmer writes: *Kapferer's study underlines the need in studies of social support to focus on the resources exchanged in the network, and exchanges, costs and rules which operate within it.*[12]

What is being exchanged? Many with learning difficulties do not, on the surface, have much to exchange. Furthermore, some exchanges (eg, involving deference or independence) may be to their disadvantage. Jean Vanier takes a more positive view: *One of the most precious gifts in a community is to be found among the people who cannot assume important responsibilities. They have no ability to organise, inspire, look ahead or command, but they have very sensitive and loving hearts. They can recognise people in difficulty straightaway and, with a smile, a look, a flower or a word, make these people feel that they are close to them, carrying their cross for them. These insignificant people are at the heart of the community and carry its extremes as well. They carry the people who are discontented, who are blocked towards each other, who are envious or disagree radically. It is the love of the hidden people which keeps the community united. The leader brings unity through justice, but these loving people are creators of unity just by being who they are. In their tenderness, they are artisans of peace.*[13]

Some may feel Jean Vanier is too romantic about what even severely disabled people can give but the extent to which relationships can be reciprocal, even with severely disabled people, is a critical element in how enduring the relationship is.

The hypothesis

If people with learning difficulties are to lead fulfilled lives they should experience a range of relationships to meet the range of basic human emotional and cognitive needs on the lines set out by Weiss. Where there is a vacuum in that range, especially at the level meeting the need for 'belonging and attachment', inappropriate transfers of behaviour from that level to other levels may occur. A person who lacks a relationship meeting the need for 'belonging and attachment' may pay a high price in personal anguish.

This range of relationships cannot exist in a vacuum and needs appropriate structures to support it. Relationships should always be considered in the context of the necessary supporting structures. Both the range of relationships and the structures which support them will need sustaining and developing.

References
1. Atkinson, D. and Ward, L. (1986) Mental Handicap: Patterns for Living: A Skills Workbook, Milton Keynes: Open University Press, p.7.
2. Weiss, R.S. (1975) The provisions of social relationships. In: Rubin, Z. (ed) Doing unto others, Englewood Cliffs, N.J, Prentice Hall, p.21.
3. Bulmer, M. (1987) The Social Basis of Community Care, London: Allen & Unwin, p.144.
4. Atkinson, D. and Ward, L. (1986) Mental Handicap: Patterns for Living: Book I, Living and Learning, Milton Keynes: Open University, p.21.
5. O'Brien, J. and Lyle, C. (1987) Framework for Accomplishment, Decatur, Ga, USA: Responsive Systems Associates.
6. Ref. 4, p.22.
7. Ref. 3, p.145.
8. Flynn, M.C. (1989) Independent Living for adults with mental handicaps: A Place of Our Own, London: Cassel, p.73.
9. Atkinson, Dorothy and Williams, P. (1990) Mental Handicap: Changing Perspectives: Workbook 2: Networks, Milton Keynes: Open University Press, p.68.
10. Ref. 4, pp. 26-27.
11. Flynn, M. and Hirst, M. (1992) This Year, Next Year, Sometime....? Learning Disability and Adulthood, London: National Development Team, p.69.
12. Ref. 3 p.134.
13. Vanier, J. (1979) Community and Growth, London: Darton, Longman and Todd, p.197.

Chapter III
Needs, structures and relationships

When I told my mother I was in a woman's group she said I was a girl. I said I was a woman. Now she knows I was right. (Women's Group: Mill Hill, London)

At the end of Chapter I, I suggested I had been working with an inadequate theoretical model. In the last chapter, I described how my experience of the project suggested a more adequate one. The central belief is that there is a range of human emotional and cognitive needs which must be met if life is to be worth living. Not all are equal, but all are important. These needs can only be met through appropriate relationships which require a suitable setting or settings to develop (ie. relationships to meet human needs must be considered within the structures or settings which support them). This can be represented by a matrix relating the two (Figure 1, p33).

The four areas under structural factors (residence/home, work/education/occupation, leisure/social/spiritual and supportive services and people) were discussed in the previous chapter. The matrix shows that the relevant relationship occurs at the intersection of the needs and the structure: thus the need for belonging and attachment may well be met in the home by a spouse; the need for social integration by friendly people in a church; the need to give nurturance by looking after a young nephew or niece on a weekly visit to a married sister; the need for reassurance of worth in a workplace by sympathetic fellow employees and a good boss; the need for exercise of choice by taking a regular shopping expedition with a support worker or relative; the need for reliable assistance by a team of home helps; the need for guidance by respected others from a volunteer at Mencap or a social worker.

Structural factors (ie. settings or occasions)
A relationship may develop in one setting but continue away from that setting or after the person concerned has left. The project showed this to be important. Places where people previously lived, especially hospitals and hostels, were highly significant for past, present and potential relationships, as were the adult training centres where many had spent a lot of time. David Brandon made this point: *Former patients are frequently ambivalent about moving out into the community. They*

might have hated the institutions but they missed the people. Huge chunks of their lives were spent there with large emotional investments. Most people they have grown to know intimately lived there and are now scattered... Financial and management considerations still dominate placements. They are separated from people, both staff and residents, who had been regarded as close friends.[1]

So far I have concentrated on the range of human emotional and cognitive needs and the relationships needed to meet them. Although I have referred to the importance of structures I have not discussed them in detail. Chapters III - VII look at how different relationships developed in various structures or settings – and, sometimes, what stopped them developing.

From an examination of actual or potential relationships relative to a particular setting, three main groups emerged, though not all are present in every setting. They are:
• relationships with others with learning difficulties
• relationships with staff, or former members of staff
• relationships with other non-disabled people.

Figure 1 divides this up as: Residence/Home; Work/Education/Occupation; Leisure/Social/ Spiritual; Supportive Services and People. However, the data fitted more easily into the less tidy division I have adopted in the following chapters. One factor is what I call 'the weight of time'.

An overwhelming impression from the project was that many people with learning difficulties find time a burden not a gift – whether it was Arthur Needles watching television all day in the sitting room at his parents' house, Christopher Johnson lying on the sitting room floor playing with his sock, or Philip Brindley and Jason Havering in their pleasant house watching television programmes which did not interest them. People at the big training centres spent all day in 'leisure' pursuits which had replaced more meaningful activities. At the poorly staffed hostel people wandered aimlessly, one man spending most of the time on his bed, masturbating.

Time was a burden for far too many. Time, relationships and structures all go together. We have much to learn about how we can enable people to structure time so it is a friend and not an enemy. 'Spare'

Continued on page 34

Structural Factors ie. Settings or Occasions

Structural Factors ie. Settings or Occasions	Basic Human Emotional and Cognitive Needs						
	Belonging and attachment	Social integration	Nurturance	Reassurance of worth	Exercise of choice	Reliable assistance	Guidance from respected others
Residence/Home	Relationship with spouse		Relationship with young nephew & nieces				
Work/Education/Occupation				Relationships with workmates			
Leisure/Social/Spiritual		Relationships with people at church or in club		Friendships at snooker club			
Supportive Services and People					Going shopping with support worker	Relationships with home helps	Relationship with social worker

The relationships occur where needs and structural factors (ie. settings or occasions) intersect. The examples in the figure come mostly from p.31.

Figure 1. Needs, structures and relationships

time makes no sense for people who have no worthwhile occupation.

In my conversations with people with learning difficulties, the settings which had obviously been important for the development of relationships kept coming up – the old mental handicap hospitals, hostels and training centres. Only two people had jobs outside training centres. I grouped residential with day settings because people saw them in the same light. The shared feature is the sheer number of hours and years people spend there and it is understandable that, despite their negative image, they were important for the development of relationships. Hospitals, hostels and places of work are examined in Chapter IV.

In Chapter V, I examine the non-official places where people live in the community, especially the parental home, and the pressures this brings to bear on people's relationships and their attempts to extend or develop them. I also look at what happened to those who left the parental home at different stages of their lives and the impact this had on their relationships.

Chapter VI covers both Leisure/Social/Spiritual and Supportive Services and Supportive People. Chapter VII is a summary of what has been learnt about the way needs and relationships relate to structures.

Reference
1. Brandon, D. (1992) Must moving out mean moving on? *Community Living*, Vol.5, No.4, April 1992, p.18.

Chapter IV
Hospitals, hostels and the workplace

I like to help out on the military pins. Somebody counts the pins and puts them in the bags. I staple the bags to the cardboard. Tommy Prince packs them into little boxes. Doreen Cochlin puts them into big boxes and puts them into the stock room. (Linda, William Brinson Centre, London)

I'm no good now, am I? I'm on the scrap heap. There's nowt to do now. They've sold all the machines. It's not like it used to be. (Woodfold ATC., Sheffield)

I've got friends where I live at the hostel. When I move I'll still visit them. (Speaking for Ourselves class: City Lit, London)

The workplace was almost always an adult training centre. This chapter shows that past locations could often be as important as those at the time of the project. This chapter follows the pattern of looking first at contacts with present or former residents or workmates, then at contacts with present or former staff members, and finally at relationships developed with non-disabled people, other than members of staff.

Present or former residents or workmates
Douglas Trinder, a big man in his late twenties, could play snooker and football but tired easily. His social skills were rather limited and weren't helped by his loud voice. He lived with his parents and went to a training centre five days a week. His mother said he had lots of acquaintances but no friends.

Peter Akers also lived with his parents. Once he knew you he turned his back on you while speaking. His key worker described him as 'a bit of a loner'. The training centre had not apparently generated significant relationships for Peter or Douglas, though attendance may have enhanced their 'reassurance of worth'.

This was certainly the case for Dennis Jones who lived in a small staffed group home and went to an industrial unit which re-cycled paper. He was immensely proud of his proper job and of earning a wage. He valued catching a bus in the morning like any other working man, buying the *Sun* on his way to the bus stop, sniggering with other men over page three and coming home having done a proper man's job. He was well integrated with his fellow workers and the recent move to this job (from a training centre) had boosted his self-esteem enormously. He did not contact his workmates outside working hours and tended to keep his own company at home. Although there was no sign that any relationships at work were likely to develop into a deeper friendship, they met Dennis's needs for 'social integration' and 'reassurance of worth'. The regularity and routine of the job also helped give a much needed framework and structure to his life.

Brian Attwell's experience is in marked contrast. He lived at the same small staffed group home and had attended a big adult training centre where industrial contract work used to be carried out. He had derived great satisfaction from this work and felt he was doing real work; indeed he was, even though he was not paid a real wage. This was then decreed exploitative and stopped; 'recreational activities' were all that were left. Brian's sense of himself as a working man, who could hold his head up, was demolished. He found it hard to accept 'leisure' during working hours since he feels work is for work time. Those responsible for the changes saw only exploitation and failed to ask themselves or those concerned what that work meant to those doing it. Perhaps they would have acted more sensitively if they had understood better the contribution that work, and the relationships that went with it, made to people's sense of identity.

Felicity Broadhurst and Hilary Fenton, both in their early thirties, attended an industrial training unit. Following encouragement and support by their parents, they chose to live in their own flats. They became friends and, most unusually, met outside working hours. Occasionally they visited each other's flats and also took part, outside work, in an informal group run by Victor Gentle (described below, p55). Most of the weekday meetings were at the industrial unit which, together with Victor Gentle's group, provided the structure to maintain the young women's friendship. Without that support the friendship might have faded away. It contributed to their 'social integration' and 'reassurance of worth', probably also to 'nurturance' in their concern for one another. It also met some of their need for 'belonging and attachment'.

Some of the relationships and friendships described so far proved remarkably resilient, despite having been born in the unpromising environment of a mental handicap hospital or hostel. People should be given the opportunity to maintain those friendships. Friendships between people with learning difficulties are all too frequently ended, arbitrarily and suddenly, by a move away. Valued relationships, started in a hostel, should where possible be restored after people move into their own homes nearby. Local networks can provide a source of considerable mutual support.

John Edwards lived in a flat by himself. He seemed self-contained but kept on referring to people he knew in the hostel he lived in eight years previously. It proved impossible to trace the person he mentioned most often but one day, out of the blue, he mentioned Henry Potts whom I knew lived on the other side of the town in a staffed residence. I established that Henry would like to see him again and drove him across. They appeared to enjoy one another's company and expressed an interest in meeting again. If the relationship was to flourish they had to meet under their own steam. Unfortunately, the journey involved two buses and the stop outside Henry's home was not easy to spot. John had a day job with normal working hours; Henry liked travelling by bus or train, but was usually back by early evening. John therefore had to learn how to use the buses in the evening. Henry had no phone and could not tell the time so timed appointments could not be guaranteed. It was best that John just went, hoping Henry would be in. The first attempt was frustrated by a burst water main – no buses. The second and third succeeded.

By the end of the fourth journey John had managed the whole journey except for the final stop but this was becoming easier as the evenings got lighter. However, because of the lighter evenings Henry returned later and was out when John arrived. We were assured by a staff member that Henry did not usually go out on Sundays but this was not a good day for me and it was six weeks before I could manage one. Unfortunately, the bus travelled by a different route and John was still unable to recognise the final stop. We reckoned it would take at least one more Sunday trip before he could be certain of where to get off. I arranged for him to leave his flat at 1.30 pm on Sunday and meet Henry at the bus station from which the second bus left. As John could not tell the time we chose a Sunday when the home care worker, who knew John well, was on duty. (She worked every other weekend). She was to call on John before she went off duty at 1.30 and tell him it was time to go. In the event, John did not wait and arrived at Henry's flat just as Henry was setting off to meet him at the bus station.

There were still hiccups, such as when the home care worker was not told John would be spending a weekend with a family. But it usually worked well. It met a need John had expressed and Henry seemed comfortable meeting John. The role of the workers on both sides was important and the link would not have been made without their energetic and concerned co-operation. Both John and Henry were people to whom it was not easy to relate and it was particularly satisfactory that they related to one another so well. John's other significant contacts were van drivers in the local authority delivery service, where he worked in a voluntary capacity, and his home care worker. Henry was a loner and spent much of his time travelling by himself on trains and buses. It is hard to classify what he got out of this relationship in terms of the typology in Figure 1 but easy to see its value.

The story of Christopher Johnson and the ultimately vain attempt to re-unite him with his friend Mary Cartwright has been told above (pp25-26). Another example shows the difficulties of trying to enable such reunions. Anthony Turner, who was over retirement age, lived alone on the seventh floor of a tower block. He still went to day care five days a week but was very lonely in the evenings and was keen to have visitors. Brian Attwell, who was so put out when industrial work was stopped in his training centre, lived in a staffed house a short bus ride away. He was in his fifties and very sociable. We discovered they had known each other at a hostel and, yes, they would both like to meet again. Brian felt it would not be satisfactory to meet in the staffed house so it would have to be at Anthony's flat. But there was an entryphone and Brian could not deal with numbers. The first time a member of staff took Brian up and it worked fine. The next time Anthony was out. The day centre had not reminded Anthony on the day itself that Brian was coming and he had forgotten. It was agreed Anthony would be reminded on the day and that Brian would go round to the tower block by himself. Anthony would look out for him and would let him in. Despite several attempts it never worked. The best solution would have had Brian ringing up before he set out. But Anthony had no phone, certainly couldn't afford one and it was unlikely the social services would agree to install one. What price friendship? I arranged a meeting to explore this.

Present at this meeting were Anthony, the key worker from his day centre to whom he was very attached and who played a critical part in his life, practically and emotionally, Anthony's social worker, Brian Attwell, the person in charge of the small staffed group home in which Brian lived who was also critical in holding his life together, and myself. Suddenly all problems melted away. In about 20 minutes it was agreed that on Mondays Anthony, instead of going back to his flat, would have his tea in the staffed house with Brian and the other four residents. Anthony and Brian would then catch the bus together and spend the evening at Anthony's flat. Brian would then catch the bus back. It worked like clockwork. A free cooked tea was an additional incentive for Anthony and both evidently enjoyed each other's company. It was particularly important for Brian. The rest of his life was in some upheaval; spending an evening with someone from his past apparently created an oasis of security which he badly needed. Note that the relationship was supported by two workers who knew their clients extremely well and cared about them.

These examples illustrate more or less successful attempts to restore interrupted friendships. In the next example two friends were together at the start of the project but have since been separated. Michael Preston was a quiet man in his forties who lived with his widowed mother. His relationship with her was good and he seemed content at home, though he had virtually no other social contacts there. He went to a training centre five days a week. When I asked what he enjoyed doing most he didn't answer. His key worker said his response to this question at an individual programme meeting had been: "Sitting next to June". It emerged that he and June Haston had a close, stable and deeply satisfying relationship. All who knew them said that it was an unusually mature relationship, obviously important to both.

I found Michael had had a good relationship at that training centre with someone else who had been moved two years ago to another centre. The relationship with June developed after that. Unfortunately, the relationship between Michael and June was in its turn under threat because Michael was due to be moved to a day centre closer to home. In view of the importance of this relationship and the way in which all concerned were quite clear about its value, I helped Michael's mother and June's mother write to the head of the day centre asking to preserve the status quo. There was no realistic prospect of maintaining the friendship outside the day centre because of distance. Neither family had transport and neither June nor Michael could travel alone.

Some assurances were received that, if Michael moved, arrangements would be made for him to return to the centre for coffee a couple of days a week. To prepare for this we set up a meeting between Michael and June, their key workers at the day centre and myself. This proved most frustrating because neither Michael nor June would say unequivocally that they did not want to move – whether from a desire to please those in authority, a reluctance to be assertive, or an inability to recognise their real wishes.

Three months later, it was not Michael who moved but June, apparently the result of a policy decision that people from a given area should attend the same training centre, although the new centre was no closer to June's home. A concession enabled June to meet Michael at the original centre once a week. I discovered there was a possibility that Michael and June might also meet weekly at a club two miles away from each of the centres. Transport linked the club with Michael's centre but there was no similar link for June. Fortunately, I found a volunteer to take June, which meant that Michael and June could meet one and a half days a week, if they were lucky.

Then Michael's long-awaited move to the centre close to his home took place. The volunteer was not informed and continued to take June to the club because she enjoyed it and found it stimulating. Michael continued to meet June weekly at the old centre but transport was being reorganised on a localised basis, creating a real danger that the meetings would end.

In this confusing sequence I found it hard to know whom to contact, when, to achieve what. When Michael and June were split up neither went into decline nor did they obviously grieve the loss of each other's company. They were glad to meet but did not seem desperately upset when this did not happen. This could be taken as a justification for having ignored what was obviously an important friendship. Difficulties were enhanced by their unwillingness to say unequivocally they did not want to be moved on any account, and further complicated by the fact that both mothers were inclined to respect authority and were not prepared to assert the wishes of their son or daughter. More recently the transport and other arrangements repeatedly broke down and the friendship has withered. Before long there may not be a friendship left to save.

In what frame of mind did those in authority approach this situation? Did they say: 'We're going to make some administrative changes and we might allow a few concessions to the friendships we know about'.? Or do planners accept that friendships of people with learning difficulties are precious and fragile and need to be encouraged if at all possible? There seems to have been no sense of responsibility on the part of those in authority towards a friendship that was important and of great potential to two people, which was likely to be fragile, and which should have been central to any planning for these people. It almost appears as if those in authority are now able to say, 'Why were you making so much fuss? You can see it wasn't so important after all'. Breaking up this friendship may not cause Michael and June too much distress, but is that the point? The challenge was to recognise something precious and to encourage and nurture it. There was no doubt that this relationship met the needs of both of them for a sense of 'belonging and attachment'.

In fairness it should be added that those responsible for the moves took a different view of the situation and felt they had taken all steps they reasonably could to maintain the friendship.

Other situations have had more satisfactory outcomes. When Freda and Geoffrey Parker met at a training centre he was living with his family and she was developing her living skills in a hostel. When they announced they wanted to get married their families opposed this. Staff at both the hostel and the training centre were most supportive and it was a hostel staff member who took the place of Freda's father and gave her away at the wedding.

Mavis and Simon West met at a hostel. They found dealing with money, shopping and cooking quite difficult. When it became clear they wanted to get married there was concern that Mavis could not manage the drugs for her quite severe epilepsy. They moved into a flat of their own and, each day, Mavis visited the hostel, only ten minutes walk away, to get her drugs. Eighteen months later she was able to manage her drugs independently. The couple's ability to cope with household finances also improved greatly.

How these people coped subsequently is discussed below. The point is that in these examples a hostel, a training centre, or a combination of both, provided the structure within which relationships were able to develop. The staff were heavily involved in providing training and support. The progression of the relationships from one 'in which participants share concerns because they are in the same situation' (part of Weiss' description of 'social integration') to one of 'belonging and attachment' owes a great deal to the structure within which it took place.

Residence and workplace are important as a source of significant relationships and it is vital that those with power over people with learning difficulties should respect and honour existing relationships and do everything possible to strengthen and support them. If one aim is to give people more choice there is no better place to start than in respecting the choice of friends they have made already.

Many relationships which have given the greatest sense of being valued (ie. where people have married or chosen to live together) started in hostels or training centres. Plans to phase out hostels and the larger centres have much to commend them but it is worth asking where people with learning difficulties will then have the opportunity to meet those most likely to form intimate relationships with them?

Present and former members of staff

Through their many hours of contact, some members of staff play a central role in the lives of people with learning difficulties in hostels or training centres. Many have worked in the same place for over five years and have had the opportunity to get to know some of the people with learning difficulties really well. Obviously some staff members have grasped this opportunity, especially in the role of key worker.

This was obvious in the case of Anthony Turner, mentioned above. His key worker understood him very well and he trusted her. She had become a vital part of his 'structure of living', helping him deal with bills, letters, problems and phone calls, in a way which enhanced his independence. She provided 'reliable assistance'. When it was suggested that he might like to move to a centre closer to his flat, he reacted very strongly, the main reason seemingly that he would lose contact with his key worker. A sensible compromise enabled him to remain in touch by spending some time at his old centre while making more contacts locally at a centre near to where he lived.

Staff members can play a critical role because of the position they have within the structure of the lives of people with learning difficulties. Day care staff are usually in touch with those who attend for most of the working week – a very different situation from that of social workers. They are well placed, if they can make the time, to develop the structure. Look at the part that Anthony Turner's key worker played in reforging the link with Brian Attwell (pp38-39). Eventually all she had to do was remind him it was Monday, the day he had tea with Brian, a simple matter but its effect for good on the relationship and wellbeing of two people was considerable. It was similar with the person in charge of the group home where Brian lived; first suggesting that Anthony could have his tea there, then providing it.

The importance of this can be appreciated better when the structure and routine of day care, with its links into other services and its committed staff members, is compared with the isolated position of others with learning difficulties, especially those living at home. The failure to re-establish the friendship between Christopher Johnson and Mary Cartwright (pp25-26) was largely due to a lack of firm and reliable structure in Christopher's life onto which I could fasten. There was no competent or reliable person who could ensure that what had been agreed would happen. This may seem critical of Christopher's mother but it simply recognises she was fully committed to caring for him and did not have the energy or the resources (eg. a telephone) for anything beyond a basic and tolerably satisfactory routine.

Good working relationships with day care staff often enabled me to make a link between a volunteer and a person with learning difficulties. The staff member and the structure of day care provided a definable slot into which the volunteer could fit and the means for giving the volunteer necessary support. Examples can be seen below in those who were linked with Arnold Trapman (p48) and James Pearson (p48).

Such members of staff often become very attached to those for whom they have responsibility. As Atkinson put it: 'The closeness, the informality and the long term nature of the contact, led sometimes to friendship, to reciprocal relationships developing between some social workers and some service users'.[1] It is important to recognise that reality, but it is also important to recognise that a person's social network and sense of self-esteem are at risk if all the people they count as friends are 'paid friends'. This is the strongest incentive for staff to use their strategic position to enable people with learning difficulties to develop other friendships. Low staffing levels and lack of time make this difficult. It was significant that when I appeared and offered an extra resource to develop such links, several members of day care and residential staff seized the opportunity. There are major implications here, not just for training but also for resources.

More positively, retired staff members who have worked at hostels and day centres may welcome the chance to become friends with a person with learning difficulties but without the problem of being paid. Instead of sharing their attention they would be able to devote it to one person. Two retired staff members did show an interest. One linked up with a man he did not know previously; the other did the opposite, linking up with an older man from the hostel where she used to work.

Relationships with non-handicapped people

Friendships formed and maintained in training centres are bound to be with others with learning difficulties or, occasionally, with members of staff. Such friendships should be valued but a job in open or semi-open employment gives wider opportunities.

Only one, among all I contacted, had an ordinary job. Geoff Price, a contract gardener, did not mention that any of the gang of four gardeners were particular friends but he seemed content with his job. Dennis Jones had a form of sheltered employment which suited him (pp35-36) and was a huge improvement on the training centre. John Edwards worked voluntarily five days a week with local authority delivery vans, as mentioned. A year or so previously he left this 'work' because of difficulties with one of the drivers and got a very dirty and unpleasant job in a sheet metal firm. He gave this up because he disliked it so much and, after unsatisfactory work experiences, went back to the local authority delivery service entirely on his own initiative. He seemed content with this occupation.

Jobs are difficult to find, particularly when the economy of the country is depressed but, remarkably, some supported employment projects are having considerable success. The very limited evidence from this project shows how important a job can be. It is a place where friends may be made; it is a way of spending time productively rather than boring time-wasting; earnings, an allowed top-up to benefits, or even a full wage are possible; it is a source of self-respect. Jobs are examined further in the final chapter.

Reference
1. Atkinson, Dorothy (1989) Someone to turn to: the social worker's role and the role of frontline staff in relation to people with mental handicaps, Kidderminster: BIMH Publications.

Chapter V
Living at home

My mum's done a lot for me. I always think I'm the worst one of the lot, but I'm not. I'm a great help to my mum with the cooking and the washing up.

My family means a lot to me. They torment me with food at Christmas time, telling me to have more.

I think of my dad at Christmas, wishing he was here. It brings a lump to my throat. (Linda Collins: William Brinson Centre, London)

This section, and the one that follows, examine the impact living situations have on people's network of relationships, particularly their need for 'belonging and attachment'. For almost everyone there is a period when this need is met by parents. Later, it is normally, though not invariably, met by other people, perhaps a partner or close friend. The central theme is that because this transfer often does not occur for people with learning difficulties, tension develops between them and their parents. Beyond this, the death of parents can leave people with learning difficulties in a vulnerable position, especially emotionally.

Living with parents: all right...

Josie Banner, in her early twenties, could do little for herself but had a happy temperament and appeared to be living contentedly with her family. It seemed her parents met her need for a sense of 'belonging and attachment' and that her family had managed to put together a structure which gave everyone in it a sense of wellbeing, even if life was somewhat restricted. The elements included a good day centre, regular respite care once a month in a small hostel where Josie was known and her mother knew she was happy (she could not talk), regular visits from a community nurse whom Josie trusted and a lot of support from her brother, sister and aunt. Her mother added: "We've always had good neighbours. They are there when you need them but are not always in the house."

A key question, always, is what happens when parents die. In Josie's case she would probably enter her short-term care hostel (assuming it is open) where she had formed some good relationships with the staff. In addition her brother and sister will probably be around to maintain their links with her. Within its limitations the structure of Josie's life and that of her parents seemed 'good enough' (to adapt Winnicott's phrase: 'good enough parenting'). Admittedly, her existence was rather segregated and she had limited social relationships but, judged in terms of a sense of well-being, it was not bad. It depended heavily and appropriately on statutory services but they seemed to work well and by and large Josie appeared content.

Living with parents: all right BUT....

By comparison, Christopher Johnson's situation, described above (pp25-26) was far more fragile. His need for 'belonging and attachment' appeared to be abundantly supplied by his mother, but his dependence on her was virtually total. In view of this, the failure to re-establish the link with Mary Cartwright was particularly sad. In terms of structure Christopher Johnson's situation was that of entropic collapse (ie. it had collapsed to its most basic state), requiring treatment as a 'relationship emergency' *before* his mother became ill or died and Christopher had to be taken to some form of care where he knew nobody. It is pointless to imagine this could be done by anyone but the statutory services or an agency funded by them. There was a need for a basic framework of services in which it might be possible to (a) re-link him with Mary Cartwright, and (b) create a setting in which a volunteer or, preferably, volunteers, might establish a relationship with him. However, achieving the latter option was likely to be easier and more effective if based on his warm relationship with Mary Cartwright, using her zest as a way of enriching his life.

Living with parents: all right and developing relationships...

Jennifer Morton's parents and the statutory services had created a structure which not only increased her choice and opportunities but recognised her parents' mortality and looked to the future. She was in her early twenties, was confined to a wheelchair, could read and write a bit and was learning to use a word processor. She went to two different day care settings, one she found stimulating, the other not. The word processing work was done at college once a week. She had some friends at a PHAB (Physically Handicapped Able Bodied) club, attended an ordinary youth club twice a week and a disco at the training centre once a fortnight. On Saturdays she visited her grandma, often rang up her favourite aunt during the week, and saw quite a lot of the wider family throughout the year.

This structure allowed her to maintain and develop a range of relationships. The basic provision during the working week had been set up with the help of a social worker at a time when things were going badly after Jennifer had left school. It had paid handsome dividends especially in terms of Jennifer's sense of self-worth. The social worker had given invaluable 'reliable assistance' and 'guidance' when her parents were uncertain how to respond.

Her parents were central to Jennifer's life and were almost certainly her most important relationship (ie. they met her need for 'belonging and attachment'). They were also fit, had a car and were good organisers. Jennifer's comparatively varied and integrated social life would have collapsed without her parents' car. It was also important that her parents were fit enough to lift her and knew how to do so.

The structure gave Jennifer opportunities for friendships which might develop, provided existing structures were maintained and her parents remained healthy and fit. (They were good 'care managers').

Living with parents: strains appearing...

Unsurprisingly, strains had begun to appear in the relationships of a large number of people living with their parents. The people I mention here did not give the impression they had grown out of the sense of 'belonging and attachment' given by their parents but there were signs that the process was under way. Peter Akers' primary relationship and main sense of attachment appeared to be with his parents (p35). He was in his twenties and his mother was heavily involved with the local Mencap. He regularly attended the Gateway Club but never had anything to do with his mother there, preferring instead to show his independence. Having got to know two young men at the club he invited them home to tea on his birthday. Afterwards, his guests suggested that Peter and his parents should accompany them to a working men's club. The Akers enjoyed the entertainment so much they joined the club and continued to go there with Peter and to meet the two friends.

Peter quite enjoyed his training centre but his range of relationships was rather restricted. He was passionately interested in trainspotting and very knowledgeable about it but an attempt to link up with a spotter group failed due to the lack (rather to my surprise) of such a group locally. Peter's abilities and opportunities for developing relationships – especially close ones – were very limited and were not helped by his habit of turning his back when talking to anyone he knew well.

Douglas Trinder, mentioned above (p35), could talk quite well and look after himself. He was keen on sports and enjoyed snooker at the Gateway Club. He played bowls and football and swam regularly. On Sunday he accompanied his parents to the pub where he played darts and was well accepted. But he had a very loud voice. When told to speak quietly, he could manage it for one sentence and then be up to full volume again, hindering the formation of close relationships. His mother said: "He does not get close to people of his own age". His key worker at the training centre, which he attended five days a week, said he had one friend but they were trying to dissuade Douglas from putting his hands inside her clothes.

Perhaps Douglas could be helped to develop social skills but it is an open question about how often he would be able to use them. He was still very dependent on his mother: during a week spent at a hostel for respite care, he would refuse to open his bowels until he returned home.. He had a wide range of acquaintances through the training centre and Gateway but his sense of 'belonging and attachment' appeared to be focused almost entirely on his parents, especially his mother. Because he was very interested in buses I thought it might be possible to use this as a link outside his segregated life style but I could not find a suitable group. Also, talking like a loud hailer all the time does create problems. It was hard to see how Douglas might develop a relationship to meet his need for 'belonging and attachment' in addition to that provided by his parents.

The same could be said of Arnold Trapman and James Pearson. Quite able, Arnold lived with his parents but his obsessive behaviour led them a fearful dance; for example, spending two hours in the lavatory and refusing to go to bed until two or three in the morning. Despite these difficulties, his sense of 'belonging and attachment' rested almost entirely on his parents. Although he was not good at forming relationships, and deliberately kept himself apart, he did respond to one-on-one situations, in both cases with men only a little older – a student nurse on placement and a young volunteer who contacted me. Thanks to the structure and support provided by the key worker in the small locally based day centre, Harry Evans, the volunteer, forged an excellent relationship with Arnold based on their shared love of sport, especially football. They met up once a week. This friendship seemed to be making a difference to Arnold's life, not least to his sense of self worth. It did not deal with the central issue but it could have provided some clues about how that might be tackled.

James Pearson was in his mid-thirties and lived with his elderly widowed mother. He attended training centre four days a week and college one day. Once taught, he could use several bus routes on his own. Although he could not manage money and suffered from ill health periodically, he was quite able. He never went out in the evenings or weekends. His key worker at the day centre said, "He desperately needs a companion, a man". Lack of a someone of his own ability frustrated him, she added. He could beat everyone at the training centre at snooker, and most of the staff too. It proved possible to build on this and a volunteer accompanied him once a week to a local snooker club where they played together. John Hilton, the volunteer, hoped that James would use the club he himself used. Again the training centre and James' key worker provided the structure and support that made this link work. Some support was very basic, eg. ringing up if James was away and acting as contact if John Hilton was unavailable.

When I spoke alone to James he said he would like to go out but his mum would not let him. He said, "I would like to go out with a nice lady". "Who?" I asked. "I don't mind really", he replied. This was clear evidence of his desire – albeit not very strongly expressed – for a relationship which would give him a sense of 'belonging and attachment' apart from that with his mother, a matter of urgency too since his mother was in her mid-seventies.

For both James and Arnold the outside links were valuable but did not address the task facing everyone mentioned so far in this chapter (except, perhaps, Josie Banner and Jennifer Morton). Namely, achieving a relationship which provides a sense of 'belonging and attachment', especially when parents die. Neither link established was in that category. In structural terms, it is hard to address this fundamental issue without considering a possible move out of the parental home.

Pamela Scribbens illustrates this well. She was in her early twenties, living with loving professional parents. Her father was an industrial chemist; her mother worked in a computer firm. She was quite able and had managed ordinary jobs but only for short periods before they broke down. Her social life was lived through her parents' friends, especially those of her mother, for she appeared to have none of her own. Her life was very comfortable, with few incentives to develop her undoubted gifts and to make a life and relationships for herself. This would have meant living independently with some support. She needed a structure which would encourage her to mature and grow, especially in the relationships she made.

Two key examples

Practical matters usually force parents to consider moving a son or daughter out of the parental home. As Ann Richardson and Jane Ritchie have shown, 'letting go' is often difficult.[1] Margaret Race's parents were getting on, and looking after her was becoming an increasing strain. Margaret could only help a little in the house and had no social contacts outside the family. "We are always together", her mother said. Her key worker at the training centre felt a wider social life was urgently needed. Two unfortunate experiences of respite care had led Margaret's parents subsequently to reject this.

The family did need a break and the parents were concerned about the future. Margaret was not. Having discovered the family was Catholic, if only attending church very rarely, I explored the possibility of a Catholic family providing short-term care for Margaret with a view to this becoming permanent. The process was exceedingly slow but it seemed such a family might be found. The move could well meet Margaret's need for a home after her parents were unable to care for her, establishing a relationship leading to a sense of 'belonging and attachment', and opening up social connections through the life of the parish.

Another example, already mentioned, is Michael Preston (pp39-41). This chapter's constant refrain is that, often, only parents provide the vital sense of 'belonging and attachment'. Finding that sense through relationships other than with parents is difficult. Michael Preston's mother was a widow in her late sixties and he had developed a close relationship with June Heston which appeared to give both that sense of 'belonging and attachment'. The social services effectively broke this up by moving them from the training centre they both attended so that they met only once a week, provided no hitches occurred. This sort of relationshipneeds to be nurtured because it could release many people with learning difficulties from the bleak prospect of depending solely on a relationship with parents who will probably predecease them and leave them bereft.

Living with parents: wanting another close relationship

Some people, mentioned above, showed signs of wanting a close and intimate relationship other than with their parents. They tended to be more able and were moving beyond the point where parents could meet all their needs for 'belonging and attachment'.

Glen Williams was fairly competent socially and could take the initiative. He attended college once a week and a locally based training centre on the four other days, but did not have any real friends. He was at the top of the ability level in the training centre. While quite civil, he regarded others there as a cut below him and had no wish to befriend them. Instead he made friends with the staff who, naturally, could not respond as fully as he wished.

Lutfiyya recounts something similar in his study of friendships between people with and without learning difficulties: *Kitty spoke feelingly about attempting to initiate friendships with staff at the sheltered workshops. Having asked a staff member about weekend plans, she was rebuffed with: "What's that got to do with you?" Kitty added: "And they would look at you like, well, it doesn't pertain to you."*[2]

Thus, Glen disdained one group and was effectively brushed off – in however friendly and concerned a manner – by the other. When camping with his parents he made friends with 13- or 14-year-olds which sometimes led to an exchange of letters. Understandably, as the young people grew up, this lapsed creating more disappointment. Glen's relationship with his parents was good but he was clear about wanting something deeper with someone else. It was hard to see where he would find the opportunity.

Jane Hodson, only twenty, had a father in his sixties. He put her position eloquently: "She doesn't want to be going round with me and my heart condition and my wife with her arthritis and our friends. She wants friends of her own age." His words would be echoed by many parents and people with learning difficulties, especially those who found that the Gateway Club was not what they wanted. Jane had many friends near her home but they moved away as they grew up. Jane's plaintive cry was: "Why can't I have boyfriends like them?"

Both Mark Hastings and Arthur Needles expressed the same need ((pp20-22). In all cases not only was there a desire to find a relationship which gave a sense of 'belonging and attachment' beyond that provided by parents but the relationship with the parents was also under great pressure, largely because it was having to fulfil a wider range of functions than could reasonably be expected. Someone in their twenties or thirties does not expect to receive 'reassurance of worth' from parents, nor 'reliable assistance' nor 'guidance from respected others'. Yet this was the case with most of these people and it was fundamentally, structurally and emotionally unsound.

The dilemma for this more able group was that many aspired to a romantic relationship with someone who was not disabled (eg. with the glamorous images on film and television) and did not care to associate with those who were. The relationship they hoped for was not achievable, while the one which might be reciprocated was not wanted. Not everyone's need for a sense of belonging and attachment has to be met by an intimate, romantic relationship. Some meet the need in different ways. However, a significant number of more able people I contacted wanted a close, intimate, romantic relationship.

Flynn and Hirst in their survey of 79 teenagers and young adults with learning difficulties came to a similar conclusion: *This study supplies ample evidence of the wishes of young women and men for comfortably established and maintained intimate relationships. Sadly, it also testifies to their disbelief that close fulfilling relationships will ever feature in their adult lives.*[3]

Self-advocacy might be the most helpful way of tackling this since it does not say: 'You are not disabled', which is not true. It does say: 'You are able in many ways and, however disabled you may be, you are still worthwhile. You can hold your head up and be proud of yourself'. The potential of this approach is discussed further below (pp87-89).

Drafting in a volunteer and hoping this will fulfil the need for satisfying relationships is not realistic. A good volunteer, like Jennifer Parsons who befriended Arthur Needles, can be a great help but it was she who recognised very quickly how desperately he wanted a proper girlfriend.

At home with parents for a long time: moving on to own accommodation

Matthew Exton used to live with his mother. He could do a good deal for himself and had a well developed sense of independence. However, he needed help with changing his clothes, keeping himself clean and cooking in other than a rudimentary way. His speech was very limited but those who knew him well could make out some of what he said. His relationship with his mother lurched from one violent crisis to another but both resisted fiercely suggestions that Matthew should leave home.

When she was well into her eighties, his mother died and it was assumed Matthew would go into care. However, limited speech did not prevent him from indicating where he wanted to live. Each time he was taken to a hostel he returned home. Social services took the hint and set up a scheme of family aides who visited first thing in the morning, at lunchtime and in the evening, enabling Matthew to stay at home.

His experience is interesting for two reasons. His relationships with the people in the locality were particularly important because he had lived there all his life and was known, understood and accepted. On a short walk with him I saw four passers-by greet him warmly – acquaintanceships rather than relationships perhaps, or friendly tolerance and acceptance. But one contact went beyond this. Matthew had became friends with the milkman, helping him with his deliveries while wearing a United Dairies overall. Because Matthew found it difficult to do up his laces, John the milkman did them up for him. After John moved away, Matthew began collecting up the glasses in a local pub, thanks to a sympathetic publican. He also accompanied the football pools man on his rounds for about an hour. Such acceptance and tolerance should not be underestimated. Living anywhere else, Matthew, with his slightly unusual behaviour and unkempt appearance, might have caused alarm and negative reactions. As it was, he was part of the local scene.

Contrast this with problems others faced, especially from children, in the locality. Children threw stones at Freda and Geoffrey Parker's window; other children knocked on Martin and Jenny Fry's windows. Martin and Jenny made a point of not going out when children were leaving school.

A neighbour may become a friend but this is unlikely; what most people with learning difficulties look for is tolerance and acceptance. This is a strong argument for enabling people like Matthew to continue living where they are known and is a key point in terms of structure. As a result Matthew retained a network of apparently superficial relationships which may well have encouraged a sense of 'reassurance of worth' in that people acknowledged him.

Another important aspect of Matthew's experience is his relationship with the family aides. Two lived locally and had known him all his life. One said: "Apart from us he just has acquaintances. We are everything to him and he relies on us". This could present problems: he had been known to call round as early as 5 am in the summer to ask for his cigarette money (which they handed out to him each day). In terms of a friendship which created a sense of being loved and valued, Matthew's relationships with the aides were central to his well-being, although the aides themselves also needed protection from excessive demands. Fortunately, boundaries about when he might or might not contact them had been established.

To describe the aides simply as friends may be to underestimate their role. It could be argued that they, if anyone, were providing Matthew's need for a sense of 'belonging and attachment'. A combination of long-standing local contacts and the aides' support enabled Matthew to stay at home; this was augmented by an able and committed social worker who understood the importance of local contacts and was prepared to put in time ironing out problems when they occurred.

The pattern of support, although somewhat precarious, seemed to go a fair way towards meeting Matthew's need for a sense of being valued. Garry Phillips' behaviour suggested he did not feel this. His father died when he was a teenager and he lived for many years quite contentedly with his mother. His mother died when he was in his forties and he went to live with his aunt, of whom he was very fond. Unfortunately, she died as a result of a fall in her home and Garry entered the mental handicap system, having previously managed to stay outside it. After hospital, hostel and group home he finished up in his own flat. He had had an ordinary job at one point but was now in day care where he was not at all happy.

Now in his mid-fifties he was found to be behaving lecherously towards teenage girls and cross-dressing with his mother's and aunt's clothes. When his social worker talked to him about cross-dressing he explained that he sometimes felt cold inside and put on women's clothes to make him feel warm. His social worker said Garry longed achingly for a sexual partner. The need for a sense of 'belonging and attachment' met by his mother and aunt was obviously unfulfilled. Outside residential care that need was expressed overtly through his emerging sexuality.

But not all people who, after a long period, leave the parental home for their own accommodation (directly or via residential care) find themselves in this situation. Felicity Broadhurst and Hilary Fenton were friends who met in the day care industrial unit. Both were in their mid-thirties and their parents were concerned that they should be as well established as possible when they (the parents) died. I mentioned (p36) how the parents helped them to move into their own flats. Both Felicity and Hilary tended to lack initiative and needed persistent encouragement. There were certain key elements they had in common.

- The parents consistently encouraged greater independence despite their own ambivalence towards this.
- Each daughter spent a time of preparation in the same hostel to help them move out.
- After the move from the hostel, staff continued to give support – extensively in Felicity's case.
- The fact that Felicity's flat was quite close to the hostel meant she could return for support and advice. She did this frequently after she moved out and remained in touch subsequently.
- Both sets of parents remained regularly in touch. Hilary rang her parents almost every day and Felicity, too, made regular phone calls. Both met their parents regularly but the parents only visited the flats by invitation.
- Both daughters attended the industrial unit where they met one another almost full time. This provided a background structure and source of information and advice.

Neither Hilary nor Felicity could be said to be good at making friends but the structure which had been developed enabled them to remain friends. The continuing relationship with their parents was more suitably independent but still gave invaluable support. The mere fact of living alone with some support (Hilary had a weekly home help) meant they were developing the competence and confidence to live more independent lives.

But the most exciting aspect of their networks was their membership of an informal group formed by Victor Gentle who had some experience of adult education for people with learning difficulties. The group, which was totally voluntary, created a relationship between friends who happened to have learning difficulties, and someone who neither had learning difficulties nor was a professional carer nor a member of their family. Weekly meetings had taken place for nearly five years. Some ten people, men and women, took part with a core of about five, including Felicity and Hilary, attending regularly. Group members decided what would happen – a meal together, a visit to the pub, or a meeting in someone's home. It was not a hidden social education programme but a chance for members to be themselves, away from the pressures of family or professionals. Victor said it had taken him some time "to be just me" and slough off responsibility as an adult educator. He usually enjoyed himself and found the others had a good sense of humour and were all, including him, a group of friends.

This group was important because members could develop relationships independently of services and parents. It certainly met the need for 'social integration', 'reassurance of worth' and 'nurturance' because members learned to attend to other's needs even if this was as basic as offering to buy another round in a pub. It may also have contributed to a sense of 'belonging and attachment' although relationships were not usually intimate.

How far a sense of 'belonging and attachment' was being met for Felicity and Hilary is hard to judge but both had achieved worthwhile friendships and gained from being independent of their parents.

Freda and Geoffrey Parker clearly had developed a relationship which met their need for 'belonging and attachment'; their meeting and marriage is described above (p41). Being married increased Freda's self-esteem; being referred to as Mrs Parker clearly pleased her. Both regularly attended a weekly meeting for people with learning difficulties run by the two social workers at Oldale Community Centre; here they met friends and took advice about bills, letters or troubles with children ringing the front door bell to annoy them. They also made quite good contacts among people living nearby. Both had difficulty reading and a next door neighbour helped them with letters. "She helps us out", Freda said. On occasion the neighbour also interfered and upset them, something the social worker had to sort out. Freda said she asked the woman in the bottom flat "if she wants owt from the shops" when she went shopping. During the winter "we were shovelling the snow for her". She added: "Sometimes I help old people across the road."

More importantly they had made the vital transition from dependence on parents for a sense of 'belonging and attachment' to a partner of their own age, sadly at the cost of contact with their families.

Marriage or finding a partner with whom to live is not something even the most devoted social worker can be expected to arrange. But once Freda and Geoffrey decided they wanted to get married the social worker and hostel staff helped and the weekly meeting at Oldale Community Centre provided unobtrusive continuing support. The difference this made to the quality of their lives was substantial.

Left home in childhood; went to institution

The lives of those who spent a large part of their lives with their parents differed radically from those who left home early. The former had difficulty extending relationships through which they received a sense of 'belonging and attachment' beyond their parents to others, especially of their own age. Those who left home and their parents early often had little sense of 'belonging and attachment' at all.

Those still in some sort of official care

Philip Brindley and Jason Havering had been moved out of a hospital for people with learning difficulties into a house for just the two of them. Philip was cheerful, had a winning smile and could charm anyone. Jason was more restless, always on the go and often making noises. Neither could speak. Both walked quite well but needed supervision and/or help with dressing, washing and eating. Six staff in the house gave the 24-hour care they needed.

When I started fieldwork with Philip and Jason (p11), I initially concentrated on identifying interests which would enable them to establish links and thus, hopefully, friendships in the wider community. Later I will discuss the links made for Philip and Jason with local churches. However, in terms of structure and relationships, the situation for Philip and Jason differed from that of everyone else, principally because they were almost totally isolated other than via the good contacts they had with staff members and their families. Although they used the shops and buses, and went to the pub, they met no one except Philip's mother who paid a visit every two months. Both had attended adult education classes but when I started seeing them it was holiday time, July, and classes did not restart until September.

The structural questions which needed to be asked about their relationships were more about continuity and the approach of the staff. The staff had been very stable; two had been there since the house opened and two others for over four years. They were committed and concerned, as shown by the way they involved their own families.

However, none was local, a factor which can help establish links with the neighbourhood, according to several studies. Also their training was about personal care; they had been given no idea about building up contacts in the locality. As they were totally in control of Jason and Philip, social contacts were just one big blank. Staff responded readily to ideas but they were not good at maintaining those links after I stopped working there. Structural questions centred in part on the way the health authority trained, supported and managed its staff. I decided fairly quickly that the project's aim was not to reform the health authority and concentrated instead on developing local contacts.

The most important people in Jason and Philip's lives were the staff who cared for them. Any sense of 'belonging and attachment' would have to be through them. This was difficult to judge for Jason, since the main indication seemed to be how settled he was and this varied unpredictably. Philip was much more responsive. He had become attached to an older man who had worked in the house and had had to leave for health reasons about a year previously. He had returned several times to see Philip but had stopped doing so because Philip found it so upsetting each time he left. There are no guarantees that staff would not leave and this underlined the vulnerability of people like Jason and Philip. One reason for establishing links with the churches was to see if this might result in a small network of relationships to provide the necessary continuity. Some progress was made (pp71-73) but inevitably the most significant relationships, for good or ill, are provided by those in touch for many hours every day.

When I talked to the local Methodist minister about establishing contacts for Philip and Jason, he suggested Miss Polkington, an artist in her late seventies. Seeing if Philip wanted to do something artistic proved a complete failure because he refused even to hold a pencil. But he did love Miss Polkington's music tapes. Jane Raffles, a profoundly deaf friend of Miss Polkington, proved to be extremely good at working with Philip and was very persistent with him. She managed to get him to match colours and take part in simple games. This was dynamic action for Philip since he preferred sitting down in a comfortable chair doing nothing. Andrew Trend, another member of the church who lived nearby, called for Philip, walked with him to Miss Polkington's, stayed there, then escorted him back home. I called one day, just after Philip had returned, and he was glowing with pleasure, possibly the result of having three people give him their undivided attention for an afternoon. That must have boosted his self-esteem. I asked a communication therapist to see if she could help Miss Polkington and her two colleagues. She was very impressed but had no suggestions other than that they should carry on.

An attempt to involve a nearby family failed. Wealso tried to interest Jason in a horticultural project but unfortunately the first job involved shifting manure and Jason found this less than entrancing.

Because the work with Jason and Philip started from scratch it differed from most of the other work. It also raised important questions about how the health authority trained and supported its workers.

Earlier I mentioned re-establishing Brian Attwell's friendship with Anthony Turner. Brian, in his late fifties, relied heavily on the person in charge of the small staffed group home where he lived. He tended to become very anxious especially when his routine was disturbed. When this happened he bit his fingernails down to the quick until they bled. The reassurance of being able to talk with Anthony Turner (pp38-39) about old times at the training centre they both used to attend was obviously important. Brian was still in touch with one brother but his extreme insecurity suggested he had no-one who gave him a strong enough sense of 'belonging and attachment'.

Kate Briggs, who started the round of mental handicap institutions at the age of ten, appeared to suffer a similar lack. In her early forties, she had spent over ten years in a local authority hostel which did not meet her needs and where she was unhappy. She was probably the most able person there but a desperate lack of self-esteem caused her to demand attention from staff and then not listen to what they said. She appeared to feel rejected by her parents and to have no sense of 'belonging and attachment'. It was hard to see how she could gain self-esteem in this setting. She tested how much people really liked her by being difficult; when staff understandably got cross, she proved to herself she was not worth anything. Any realistic solution had to be structural, ie. finding somewhere to live where she could receive the attention she needed, gain a sense of her own value and begin to develop proper relationships. The way this was tackled (but not solved) is described in the next chapter.

Left home in childhood: to hostel, to own house
Stan Rivers (Chapter I), Anthony Turner, whom we managed to link up again with Brian Attwell, and John Edwards, who was linked up again

with Heny Potts (pp37-38), all left home in childhood. All three echoed that sense of inner emptiness which came over so strongly from Stan Rivers. Anthony Turner, in his late sixties, was desperate for company in his flat (of which he was very proud) and greatly appreciated Brian's visits (pp38-39). John Edwards could not remember any family life and longed to be part of a family.

The limited number of people I have referred to cannot prove my suggestion that many who leave their families early will have a weak sense of 'belonging and attachment', but they indicatethat it is inherently likely.

Of course, some survive the system. Geoff Price, a cheerful man in his thirties (p44) had been right through the mental handicap system and finished up living in a small group home with two other men wlth whom he was friendly but not intimate. He was quite able and had a full time job with a small gardening firm where he worked as part of a team. He walked by himself at the weekend, regularly met a girlfriend who lived in a staffed group home on the other side of the town and had a secure home base. He played snooker every week at the Mencap centre where he had more friends. He went camping with a Mencap group. His well ordered and structured life offered a range of relationships, plus a strong sense of his own worth and value. It was a pleasure to meet him.

Left home in childhood: to hostel, living with a partner
Martin and Jenny Fry had both spent substantial periods in various mental handicap institutions since childhood. Their early histories were tumultuous, especially Jenny's. She had had a difficult family background. The files spoke of temper tantrums and slovenliness and, especially, relationships with men! Anxious case conferences were held and long letters written before it was accepted that Martin and Jenny really wanted to live together and were not going to be thwarted. Neither was good with money but it was not felt to be sufficient reason for preventing the marriage, rather something which required help. When I saw them they had lived together for about four years and their relationship had improved dramatically. They needed quite a lot of help. For two hours a day, five days a week, a home aide helped with budgeting and shopping. As a result they had built up a structure which gave them a variety of relationships and interests. Martin, a great snooker player, was one of the group of quite able men who met regularly to play at the Gateway Club. He was also a member of a commercial club which he attended three times a week and where he appeared well accepted. He showed me cups he had won in tourna-

ments. Gateway was also part of Jenny's week and she played bingo there twice a week. She went alone to her mother's once a week and both visited Martin's parents each weekend. They had a settled housework routine with Martin doing the Hoovering. Jenny said proudly of herself: "I am a housewife".

In view of Martin and Jenny's early history, the situation appeared remarkably settled and they seemed, with minor hiccups, to be content with each other. This depended, of course, on substantial support – ten hours a week from a home aide – especially with regard to managing money which had been a source of friction in the past. Martin and Jenny are a particularly good example of a relationship supported by a sound structure which provided the necessary sustaining.

The same is true of Mavis and Simon West (p41) and, in particular, the way hostel staff helped Mavis with her epilepsy drugs. A home help assisted them with shopping and money one morning a week and there were occasional visits to the Oldale Community Centre meeting run by the two specialist social workers, one of whom maintained contact over and above that.

In another interesting but slightly different example, Harry Vaynol and Jack Grant had developed that key relationship which provided a sense of 'belonging and attachment' for . They had been great friends in the hostel and moved out together into their own home which they had occuped for about 15 years. They needed some help, especially with money and shopping, which they received from a small team of home helps to whom they were very attached. Initially they had used the training centre and adult education classes, including one in cookery, but had recently retired. They gave the impression of leading very contented lives, enjoying the relaxed life style of those who have earned their retirement. The other strand to their lives was that they lived with Geoff Price, mentioned above, and looked after him in several ways. They prepared his tea ready for when he got back from work which may have helped fulfil their need for 'nurturance' (ie. giving care).

Here again a good structure had been built up, with the necessary sustaining. It was true Harry and Jack depended on assistance but their position, especially their emotional position, was very different from that of Matthew Exton who depended much more on his home aides, or Anthony Turner who relied so much on his key worker at the centre. Other than these 'working' relationships, neither Matthew nor

Anthony had any other potential source for a sense of 'belonging and attachment' and were thus very vulnerable. Harry and Jack did have such a relationship, which home helps supplemented and supported, and which would still be there if the home helps changed.

Interim summary about residence

This chapter has illustrated the effect living situations have on patterns of relationships, the structural implications of this, and the ways these relationships can best be sustained.

It also shows that the situation of those who live with their parents differs from that of people who left the parental home quite early in their lives. I have emphasised the obvious importance of the relationship with parents to provide a sense of 'belonging and attachment' and contrasted this with the fact that many seem to have difficulty in developing such relationships with a contemporary. As a result, the latter are emotionally vulnerable as they grow out of an over-dependent relationship with their parents and/or the parents die.

Those who left the parental home early seemed to risk a weak sense of self-identity and to lack any sense of 'belonging and attachment'. However, where they had found a partner who provided this, the situations of those who had spent a long time in the parental home and those who had left the parental home early, did not obviously differ. The vital point was that through this relationship this group avoided the emotional black hole awaiting many people with learning difficulties.

References
1. Richardson, Ann and Ritchie, Jane (1989) Letting Go: Dilemmas for parents whose son or daughter has a mental handicap, Milton Keynes: Open University Press.
2. Lutfiyyn, Z.M. (1991) A Feeling of Being Connected: friendship between people with and without learning disabilities, Disability, Handicap and Society, Vol.6., No.3., p.240.
3. Flynn, M. and Hirst, M. (1992) This Year, Next Year, Sometime....? Learning Disability and Adulthood, London: National Development Team, p.68.

Chapter VI
Leisure

We have the right to go into the community when we please and do as others do.

We need friends. We should have more places where we can meet people and make friends and do things. We want to mix with all sorts of people. We believe people shouldn't just stay at home and feel sorry for themselves and ask for pity; there's a beautiful world out there and we want to be part of it! (from Australia, USA and Britain).

The previous chapters considered two of life's basics – work and home. This chapter deals with areas of choice, notably adult education, clubs, other recreational and community facilities, and churches. Advocacy schemes and volunteer bureaux are also considered.

I mentioned how Matthew Exton was supported at home by a team of three family aides (pp52-54). This departure from the primary theme – home/residence – raised the subject of supportive services and people, as did Felicity Broadbent and Hilary Fenton's membership of Victor Gentle's group (p55). Supportive people – in this case statutory workers – are discussed here together with the benefits some people with learning difficulties enjoy from meetings held in supportive settings.

Support groups

I am referring specifically to area-based support groups set up by social workers or community nurses. In the Hillside area two specialist social workers ran a group at Oldale Community Centre attended by six to 12 people. Practical matters, such as tax forms and benefit queries, were handled. More general problems, such as children who were being a nuisance, were also discussed. The community policeman was invited to advise on possible remedies. The group enabled all this to take place in an unthreatening setting.

Perhaps more importantly it was a place where friendships could be made and maintained. One impressive feature was the way social workers encouraged people with learning difficulties to learn the skills needed for making and sustaining friendships. Often there was much to learn. How should you respond when visited in your flat: asking the visitor to come in, taking their coat, suggesting a cup of tea, sitting down together. Visitors too may need to learn what is expected; in particular, how long to stay. A vital skill for the host is to be able to indicate politely when the guest should leave. This may seem basic but social interaction can require a lot of teaching, with rehearsal playing as big a role as discussion. The resultant social skills are vital if people are to develop friendships.

Support groups can also help sort out snarled-up relationships. As a result, deeper friendships may occur, extending beyond meetings and including visits to other people's homes. John and Philippa Mason were married and very well integrated with the Hillside area. Harry Grey, in his early seventies, lived alone, received regular support from home helps, and called on John and Philippa regularly. They seemed to be close friends. John and Philippa were the centre of a small network of people with learning difficulties in the area. (John's network of relationships is one example of matrix usage in Appendix B).

A similar group – the Helden club – met in another part of town in the evening and fulfilled the same function. The resultant networks of friends were valuable for many reasons. Through the club, two brothers, Edward and Cliff Jaques, were good friends with another man, Tom Bristow. Tom's mother died, leaving him bereft and miserable. His social worker was concerned about how he would manage. Cliff volunteered to move in, stayed for about two months (their homes were not far apart), then gradually moved back to his own home.

Simultaneously, levels of day care and domestic help were increased but the key role was played by Cliff who was tolerant of Tom's rather manic behaviour. The social worker admitted he could not have tolerated Tom for more than half an hour and thought that no-one could have coped with him in the way that Cliff did. Throughout this period the social worker provided coordination, encouragement and support through regular contact with people at the Helden Club.

Brother and sister, Hilda and Frank Hessing, both had learning difficulties, with Hilda considerably less able than Frank. After their mother died they managed, with a bit of help, to continue to live in the family home. When Frank went into hospital for a few days Hilda could not look after herself and it seemed as if she would have to be admitted to care. She was not keen on this. However, a friend, Bruce Mander, whose mother had died before theirs, used to visit regularly, often staying for a meal. (Indeed the social worker had to keep an eye on this to make sure Bruce did not eat them out of house and home). He had a good relationship with Hilda, who thought the world of him, something Bruce greatly appreciated.

When Frank was in hospital it was arranged that Bruce should spend the three days with Hilda. The care was personal and friendly and in Hilda's own home. She was excited and saw it as a treat, while Bruce gained self-esteem, realising he had something to offer. He had become a giver of services. These mutual benefits were only possible because the network of relationships gave a convenient point of access for the social worker. The initial introduction was organised by the social worker and led to Hilda and Frank inviting Bruce to clean up their garden which they were unable to do. Bruce, wanting the money, agreed to do it.

The need, of course, is to see people with learning difficulties as people with resources to offer. A combination of the Helden Club and local knowledge enabled the social worker to help people widen and enrich their network of relationships. The way the more able could help the less able was particularly valuable in building up self-esteem.

However, the more able may exploit the less able. Nurturing has much to commend it but workers may at times have to protect the more vulnerable from, for example, theft.

Social workers created another important network by setting up a club where friends who had been in residential care together and had moved away were able to keep in touch. One man, who had looked after his mother for years before she died, met a woman who 'enjoyed ill health' at the club and married her. Thus two inter-dependent needs were met.

Many relationship needs – from 'belonging and attachment' to 'guidance from respected others' – are met through these support groups/clubs. Although sometimes criticised for being segregated, they can give people the confidence and support to function in the wider community and they can sustain the networks of friendship among those with learning difficulties. They also enable social workers and other professionals to link in easily and informally where help is needed.

It is likely that bonds of friendship and affection will grow between staff and those with learning difficulties since it is not a setting which encourages professional detachment. Friendships are, however, perilous for the person with learning difficulties since the professional worker may move on. Here, support groups are stronger than, say, training centres, since a primary aim is to help people develop and maintain autonomous relationships. Nevertheless, the tension remains for professional staff.

Adult education

Because adult education has been explored by several people (Jeannie Sutcliffe's Adults with Learning Difficulties: Education for Choice and Empowerment[1] is extremely helpful) I have not dealt with it in detail here. However, it is important and must be considered, albeit briefly.

Friendship between people with learning difficulties in the same class

People with learning difficulties attending adult education classes seemed to know others there with learning difficulties before they started the class. Thus, classes provided an opportunity for maintaining and possibly deepening friendships rather than making new ones.

Friendship with teachers

In my experience, those who teach classes for people with special needs or classes which include people with special needs, do so because they enjoy it and think it is important. Relations tend to be warm and supportive. I have already mentioned (p22) the important part retired teacher, Jennifer Parsons, played in Arthur Needles' life.

Friendship with class members who are not handicapped

Doreen Oates attended a cookery class which included several people with learning difficulties. This gave the class a different feel and Doreen relished this difference, taking great delight in her relationship with disabled members of the class. Friendship did not extend beyond the class. Some relationship needs in the 'social integration' category were met and there was the potential for something deeper. The class teacher said she did not know how she would have managed without Doreen's help.

Adult education, especially when not limited to formal education, may also encourage friendships since it is an accepted and valued activity, not seen as deviant. Many non-disabled people use adult education classes to meet people and make friends since the fixed agenda avoids the problem of facing someone and wondering what to say. The educational element need not be formal – just someone with knowledge or a skill (perhaps as basic and important as baking) they are glad to share and someone else who wants to learn. The carefully thought-out approach at Croft Technical College, described in the Open University Patterns for Living[2] course, is a good model for encouraging the development of friendships.

Education was not a priority in this project. Because adult education classes are split into terms and only last a year or two, they are of limited value in the development of longstanding relationships. People are likely to spend much more time in hostels or training centres.

I suspect adult education's main contribution, apart from what people learn, is the way it boosts students' self-esteem. Certainly Freda and Geoffrey Parker enjoyed the cookery course where Doreen Oates was such a help, and they showed me their course certificates with great pride.

Mencap Gateway Clubs
During my search for settings where people with learning difficulties could meet and make friends the importance of Mencap clubs became apparent.

Relationships with others who have learning difficulties
The relationships that Peter Akers developed at the Gateway Club were mentioned (p47). Some quite able people who met at the Centre regularly, often to play snooker, led well integrated lives. However, the Centre was obviously a useful part of the whole, enabling them to sustain friendships which they valued. Geoff Price, who had a regular job as a gardener with a small firm and worked as part of a small gang, was mentioned (p44.). He managed all his own affairs with minimal support from his social worker. He visited the Gateway Club three times a week, had an established group of friends there and went camping with members. He said, "I am quite useful on the camping weekends". I am sure he was and that may be one reason why the Mencap con-

nection was important to him. He knew he was useful and was valued.

A swimming club met on Saturdays and a hiking club on Sundays – times when nothing was on offer at the training centres. By regularly going swimming and hiking, Brian Attwell gained the reliable framework or structure he needed to prevent himself from becoming anxious.

Relationships with 'staff'
The inverted commas indicate that most of the staff are parents of people with learning difficulties. Some of the latter chose to confide in the people who have run the coffee bar for a number of years, perhaps because they offer a different kind of relationship from parents, other family members and paid professionals. A man whose mother had died earlier and who had recently lost his father chose the caretaker, who was fully included in the life of the centre, to take charge of his money – a good indicator of the strong bonds that can develop.

Relationships with non-disabled people
Of the many volunteers, some were short-term but one young unemployed man built up an impressive relationship with a woman who had many service needs and who obviously trusted him.

Despite the significant number of volunteers, the Gateway Club is obviously segregated and it is legitimate to question how appropriately it meets the needs of those who attend. It certainly provides 'a means for the social integration of the otherwise isolated person'. I got the impression that the men who met to play snooker probably boosted their sense of self-worth through their obvious competence (especially compared with some of the other people there). The wide range of abilities led to opportunities for 'nurturance' (ie. giving help), a good example being Geoff Price's usefulness on camping weekends. It certainly provided 'reliable assistance' to both parents and people with learning difficulties themselves. The day care filled a large gap in the statutory services. Acceptable 'guidance' was provided to several people with learning difficulties especially through parents of other people with learning difficulties. Something under 'belonging and attachment' may have emerged, judging by a gentle, affectionate relationship between a very disabled young man and an equally disabled young woman at a club meeting during the day.

I had been inclined to be sniffy about Mencap but the more I saw of it the more I realised that, despite its limitations, it met a remarkably wide range of relationship needs. Without it the lives of many people would be much poorer.

Mencap encourages longstanding relationships because it has existed a long time and has not changed much. Unlike local authority day care it is unaffected by fashion. This has a downside but the upside is the reliability and security Mencap offers. Many people – including those more able – go there having rejected formal statutory services.

Other clubs

The PHAB (physically handicapped/able bodied) Clubs are more integrated by their very constitution than the Gateway Clubs and appear to play a similar role. Jennifer Morton, a young woman in her early twenties (pp46-47), went regularly to a PHAB Club where she particularly enjoyed talking to students and obviously valued the opportunity to meet non-disabled people of the same age. She also visited an ordinary youth club which provided special transport for disabled people. Felicity Broadhurst went to a PHAB club which, her mother reckoned, 'brought her out of herself'. Certainly these clubs are valuable for some people.

General community facilities

Use of general community facilities is now properly taken for granted. People should use public transport if they can and learn to travel on it independently. Forming friendships on buses is unlikely but independent travel can contribute hugely to making and sustaining relationships.

Several people went to pubs regularly. Matthew Exton, who gathered up glasses in a pub, has been mentioned. Anthony Turner visited a pub regularly and played pool with another person with learning difficulties. Felicity Broadhurst and the others in the informal group that met around Victor Gentle often met in a pub. Matthew received a degree of acceptance through gathering glasses. For others it was simply a rendezvous for meeting existing friends, not a place where friends are made. John Edwards (pp37-38) was quite a reserved man and his speech was a bit difficult to follow. He appeared to enjoy pubs but the social interaction he experienced seemed minimal. Stephen Hardwick had a severe speech defect which made it almost impossible to understand what he was saying, though in other ways he was quite able. Visiting his local, alone, almost every evening, was an important daily routine and he valued the fact that he could pay for the drink and was accepted. But it was not a place to make friends. Many regard pubs in the same light as buses – facilities to be used rather than a means of making friends. There are exceptions. Garry Phillips, (p54) had been isolating himself but then started visiting his local where the bar staff got to know him – an important lifeline in a rather lonely existence.

Leisure interests

Leisure interests seemed an attractive route but a scheme in Cheshire, which matched my experience, found the way 'steep and thorny'. Much effort was needed to discover the leisure interests of someone with learning difficulties. Peter Akers was passionately interested in trainspotting and had an encyclopaedic memory for different engine types. His mother used to take him to the railway station on Saturday mornings but now felt too old to do this. Yet Peter needed someone with him. I imagined it would be easy to link up with a trainspotting club but these tend to stress special, quite expensive trips. Finding a club based on an interest in aeroplanes ran into similar problems which I was never able to resolve. However, in talking to a group at one of the local churches, I met a delightful woman who was a member of a flying club and who agreed to take anyone interested for a flight in her plane. This proved complex logistically but Geoffrey Palmer flew once and enjoyed himself enormously. Such flights are likely to happen only rarely because of the amount of organisation needed. (Incidentally, anyone who suffers or has suffered from epilepsy may have a fit triggered by looking through an aeroplane propeller revolving at high speed).

Stan Rivers, who introduced the book, went walking regularly with a rambling club. But I had considerable difficulty in finding a suitable club for another person and by the time I had, he was in a state of some emotional turmoil and I did not dare go ahead. Unfortunately, there was no professional or experienced person to help iron out any preliminary difficulties.

However, Martin Fry found a niche in a local snooker club, played there regularly and won several competitions (pp60-71). I had nothing to do with arranging this. According to Martin he walked into the club and a friend called Geoff had a word. Certainly Martin became firmly established.

James Pearson (p48), an enthusiastic snooker player, started playing every week at a local club with a retired man, Jim Rogers. The hope was that he might find other people to play with but this could take some time since most people visit the club with the people with whom they intend to play. In effect, you need a friend in order to go to the club, although the club can help focus a relationship. Perhaps more realistic was Jim Rogers' idea of introducing James to a club where Jim himself played regularly. Normally the pair played at a club close to the training centre that James attended.

Skill is another factor. The snooker tables at the Gateway Club helped people become reasonably proficient, and one imaginative further education class taught people how to improve their snooker. Despite this some people with learning difficulties seem to enjoy just being included in a group without playing an active part in it. Philip Brindley (pp57-59) could not speak and it was difficult to persuade him to take part in any activities. But when taken to rehearsals and, eventually, the performance of a Gilbert and Sullivan production, he obviously enjoyed it. He was not the only person who seemed to want to be accepted as part of a group while remaining on the edge of it. I suspect just being there is quite an important activity – if that is the right word – for a number of people with learning difficulties, especially some of the more disabled.

Churches

Churches were the most productive source of contacts. They have a number of significant characteristics. They are generally local; they meet every Sunday or more often; they cater for all ages; no prior qualifications or skills are needed; unlike many leisure organisations they are places where people can make friends. That said, many would still find it easier to visit a church for the first time with a friend. Finally, concern for the disadvantaged is an integral part of Christian churches' reason for existence, whether or not a given church pays attention to the fact. (No work was done with people from other faiths. It would be very interesting to do so).

Philip Brindley (pp57-59) lived with just one other person, Jason Havering, in a house owned and staffed by the health authority. I discovered he had been to the local Church of England church in the past and I contacted the vicar who was keen to help. As a result members of the house staff started taking Philip to the main Sunday service. Because staffing was tight we later arranged for a rota of people to collect Philip. This also seemed a good way of helping him establish closer relationships with a few members of the congregation. The rota broke down from time to time and I had to encourage them to persist but they always responded positively. After about two years the rota was firmly established. Philip always went for coffee after the service and there was some difficulty in getting him to leave. Obviously he enjoyed going and the rest of the congregation valued having him with them. When the health authority planned to move Philip and Jason to another house some distance away, which would have complicated church attendance, the church council wrote to express their disquiet. Fortunately the idea was dropped.

We learnt one very valuable lesson from Philip. Persuading him to leave after coffee could be such a problem that a member of the house staff would have to be called. What made things so irritating for the parishioners was that the staff member merely said, 'Come on, Philip', and he came. I had encountered a similar problem at the Gilbert and Sullivan rehearsal to which I had taken him. He enjoyed it so thoroughly that, at the end, he did not want to leave. He refused to get up or even be pulled up. In desperation, I turned the lights out. Without hesitation he got up and walked to the car. I took him the second week, but I knew I couldn't, and shouldn't, do it regularly. It needed to work without me. I had arranged for a member of the society to pick up Philip on her way there and return him on the way back. But again he refused to leave and we agreed it would be unwise to carry on until this was sorted out. Not only was this tiresome but it threatened to limit his social contacts if he always had to be accompanied by a member of staff.

I discussed with staff at the house how they might pass on their ability to get Philip to move. "It's just a question of getting to know him. He is distrustful with strangers and will not do what he is asked", they said. Then one member remembered Andrew Trend had no such problems when he brought Philip back from Miss Polkington's. Andrew revealed that on arrival he took Philip's coat off. When it was time to go, he held out the coat and said, "Time to go, Philip". No problems! It was suggested that the church warden should try taking Philip's coat when he arrived at church and get him to put it on when it was time to leave. The church warden said, 'It worked a treat'. As a result the parishioners had more confidence in involving him in other aspects of church life. He was later invited to a church barbecue which he enjoyed.

How far was this simply a superficial acquaintance with some members of the congregation? It is impossible to say except that Philip gave every appearance that he enjoyed going. In his own way he participated in the services. Given that worship is the centre of church life, Philip was part of it – the very opposite of being marginalised.

Jean Vanier, founder of L'Arche, often dwells on the important contribution and gifts people with learning difficulties bring to worship. In his writings he often speaks of 'communion': *Generally speaking communion is a sense of unity deeper than working together. It is more on the level of being, and somewhere it breaks down the barriers of loneliness and gives people a sense of freedom. It has a very deep respect of difference. It is very close to the things of God. It is frequently deepened in silence and is linked much more to the body.*[3]

This clearly has a lot to do with the sense of 'belonging and attachment', 'reassurance of worth' and much else besides. We cannot quantify the value going to church had for Philip but it could be very important, as maybe it was for his housemate Jason. Philip attended Parish Communion, the same service that Jason attended at the neighbouring Roman Catholic church, where of course it is called Mass. Jason was more lively than Philip and could make embarrassing squealing noises. For nearly a year Jason was taken to church most Sundays by members of the house staff. They sat at the back and left quickly at the end of the service. Following my discussions with the priest and members of a prayer group, an older married woman, Mrs Carter, and her family took on Jason. At church he no longer sat at the back but in the middle of the congregation, usually in the same place, where people got to know him better. He received a blessing at the communion which had not happened before. After about a year he was confirmed and started receiving communion. When he received the Host he would give a little jump (In acknowledgement? Thanks?) and then make his way back to his seat. He always went for coffee after the service and was very put out if there wasn't any. He attended many of the church's other functions and even attended the prayer group which was largely silent. The house staff said he always behaved better when he went out with Mrs Carter. He also calmed down even when he was in one of his bad, noisy moods. Sometimes he played up in church and his shoes went flying, but the priest took a robust view of this. "People have learned to duck", he said.

Of course, many people with learning difficulties, like those without, will not want to become involved with churches and these wishes must be respected. But churches are potential sources of volunteers capable of working without any suggestion that church attendance be the price of their involvement. John Rogers, who played snooker with James Pearson, was a churchgoer but he did not try to persuade James to go to church. He just enjoyed playing snooker with him.

Advocacy schemes and volunteer bureaux

Bureaux offer the person with learning difficulties a potential friend. This is in many ways an artificial approach but with skilled matching it can work very well and should not be shunned. Advocacy offices often go to some trouble to explain that they are not about 'just befriending'. However, becoming an advocate generally involves becoming a friend as well. It is unlikely that someone will need advocacy all the time, whereas the essence of friendship is that it continues. A friend who comes via advocacy or a volunteer bureau may well enable the person with learning difficulties to become involved in some community facilities or organisations. In this project no-one arrived this way but John Rogers, mentioned above, came by a similar route. He responded to an appeal for help in a town centre church.

In some schemes advocates may form relationships which make a big difference to people's lives. A member of the Sheffield Citizen Advocacy enabled two old people – he 60, she over 70 – to marry in the face of considerable opposition from the local authority.[4] Subsequently, the advocate maintained a close relationship with the couple.

There is also a need for self-advocacy as a means of building up self-confidence and self-esteem in people with learning difficulties. Self-advocacy could help people with learning difficulties to develop a range of relationships, especially 'reassurance of worth'. This would be a major contribution but this project can only underline the need, not provide evidence about how far self-advocacy can meet it. The subject is discussed further in Chapter VIII.

References
1. Sutcliffe, J. (1990) Adults with Learning Difficulties: Education for choice and empowerment, Leicester: National Institute of Adult Continuing Education.
2. Atkinson, D. and Ward, L. (1986) Mental Handicap: Patterns for Living: Book I, Living and Learning, Milton Keynes: Open University Press, pp.51-52.
3. Quoted in Spink, K. (1990) Jean Vanier and L'Arche: A Communion of Love, London: Darton, Longman and Todd, p.101.
4. Morris, P. (1988) Married, thanks to citizen Jane, The Independent, July 1988.

Chapter VII

How do relationships relate to structures?

Having reached the age of nearly 70, I am well settled here. I am of informal status, which means I am able to discharge myself if I so wish. But I want to remain where I am. I have friends all around me. What more can you want in life? (Bill Challis: Leavesden Hospital, Hertfordshire)

The last three chapters have looked at settings or structures and the way relationships developed, or did not develop, in them. In a slightly different form and order, they cover the four headings (Residence/ Home; Work/Education/Occupation; Leisure/Social/Spiritual; Support-ive services and people) outlined in Chapter II (p27), which also ap-pear in Figure 1(p33).

Key points from these chapters

Relationships were overwhelmingly influenced by the locations where people spent much of their time - where they lived, or used to live, and where they 'worked' (ie. the adult training centre for the majority). These locations were often the source of long-established relationships. De-spite their importance, such relationships were frequently broken when people were moved around the learning difficulties system. Sustaining and restoring these relationships would make a major contribution to people's sense of well-being.

Staff in residential and day care establishments, especially key work-ers in nearly daily contact, can become important figures and can quite legitimately be counted as friends. As staff may move these were perilous relationships for people with learning difficulties. However, some of these workers seemed to fulfil a key role in developing wider social contacts for those with learning difficulties.

When adults lived with their parents, the close relationship between them gave them a sense of 'belonging and attachment'. However, that often precluded the development of other relationships of similar depth – especially with people of their own age. Sometimes relationships with parents became strained because they failed to mature into rela-tionships between adults. And, of course, it was likely that parents would die first. In both cases people were in danger of being landed in an emotional black hole with no relationship giving a sense of 'belonging and attachment'.

The lives of those who left the parental home early may be even more devastated because they appeared to have little if any sense of 'belonging and attachment'. Stan Rivers is one.

Those who found partners, whether married or otherwise, usually seemed more emotionally secure, regardless of the stage of life at which they had left the parental home.

The structural implications of the latter point are important. It raises the question of where people may find a partner, an especially difficult problem for those who rejected others with learning difficulties while yearning for a romantic relationship with a 'normal' person which they were unlikely to achieve. Such relationships needed sustaining. Support groups/clubs played an effective role here and were a rich source for a wide range of relationships.

Making links via shared leisure interests proved difficult but the Mencap Gateway club was valued. Snooker at Gateway was important, providing a source of valuable relationships for a group of more able men, some of whom were well integrated into the general community. Churches offered considerable potential but often needed help and support from the services.

The structural questions that need to be asked about relationships are not complicated. The key issues are:

- How do we respect and honour choices already made while enabling people to maintain, or re-establish, existing or past relationships which they do or did find precious? That said:

- Where can people meet the range of people they want to meet?

- Where are different kinds of relationships going to develop?

- How are relationships to be maintained?

Chapter VIII
General principles and methods of working

You have to know me as I am. (Speaking for Ourselves class, City Lit, London)

In this chapter I look at the underlying principles and working methods needed to develop the relationships outlined in Chapter II. Although most would say that these are the fundamental aims of all social work, I believe practice and policy can easily be blown off course and these aims need re-asserting.

Understanding the relationship context

Failure to appreciate the relationship context can put a volunteer, organisation or worker in an impossible position. This happened with the walking club with which Mark Hastings became involved (pp20-22); it nearly happened with Jennifer Parsons, the volunteer involved with Arthur Needles (p22); it happened with the home aide looking after Sharon Barker. After she and her partner separated, Sharon invested more and more in her relationship with the family aide who found it increasingly oppressive and finally could not cope. The breakdown was not the result of a lack of practical provision – Sharon attended adult education classes and the Helden Club (p64) – but of taking insufficient account of the relationship context and an inability to handle the intensity of Sharon's emotional agony which demanded considerable resources for a short time. In the event Sharon was admitted to hospital for about three weeks.

Good examples of addressing the relationship context seriously are when a wish to live together and/or get married was recognised and acted on, as with Martin and Jenny Fry and Freda and Geoffrey Parker.

Grant, Ramcharan and McGrath view the importance of the relationship context from a slightly different angle. Their study is based on the views of three people with learning difficulties living in the community.It is worth quoting at length:

The formation of close and friendly relationships with key workers, support workers and others has already been noted. The establish-

ment of such relationships is one of the undoubted keys to the success of individual work with users and families, supporting as it does the findings from phase one of the study (Grant, McGrath and Ramcharan, 1993). *However, most people with a learning disability still live without friends of their own who are not 'paid' in some way like key workers or categories of support workers like family aides. Lessening the dependency on 'paid' helpers and friends, and enabling individuals to establish genuine reciprocal relationships with other people who may become their friends, remains a major developmental challenge. We take the view that the service system has so far paid insufficient attention to methodologies for helping users and families to build supportive and non-paid relationships with others* (Dunst et al, 1989). *Given that the long-term survival of individuals with even quite mild forms of learning disability appears to depend on a variety of benefactors with paid and unpaid roles* (Edgerton 1984), *striking a balance between the two appears to be vital.*

We were impressed by the nature of some of the ties and relationships between users on two levels. First, there were those users who seemed able to cue into the needs and wants of other users with greater ease than staff. There were occasions when they spotted someone's needs before anyone else, simply because of their familiarity with the person. Sometimes they acted as interpreters or advocates for their colleagues. Second, there were users who had developed close and friendly relationships with other users on a variety of levels. As a direct result of this we witnessed many examples of users electing to share leisure time in pursuit of common interests. Sometimes it went beyond this, for example in terms of mutual aid with things like shopping, making meals, and even decorating. Although we fully support the principle of individual planning, forms of group work designed to foster mutual aid between users, based possibly on an understanding of an individual's social network, is likely to have much to commend itself. It means much more than a commitment to the establishment of self-advocacy groups, important though this is.[1]

Brechin and Swain have also made the same point forcibly in connection with the relative priorities of social skills and personal relationships: *We would question the idea that social skills are an essential foundation in personal relationships... We would argue that personal relationships and the circumstances in which people create and sustain relationships are an essential foundation for learning and applying social skills.*[2]

Grant, Ramcharan and McGrath mention that 'the social system has so far paid insufficient attention to methodologies for helping users and families to build supportive and non-paid relationships with others'. Brechin and Swain refer to 'the circumstances in which people create and nurture relationships'. This is examined in the next section.

Understanding the structural context

When I started working with Christopher Johnson I did not allow sufficiently for the fact that his support structure, and his mother's, had collapsed almost completely. As a result my efforts ran into the sand (pp25-26). The same nearly occurred with Arthur Needles (p22). On the other hand, despite his occasional very difficult behaviour, a successful link was established between Arnold Trapman and a young volunteer, largely because of the structure provided by the local day centre he attended and support from the centre's workers.

The link between Anthony Turner and Brian Attwell was re-established because of support provided by Anthony's day centre, his key worker and the person in charge of the small group home where Brian lived (see p38-39).

Kate Briggs highlights the importance of being aware of the relationship and the structural context. Kate's sense of emotional deprivation was very marked. The staff at her (excellent) local day centre initially suggested she would benefit from a volunteer who would help her sing (something she enjoys; she has a good voice and a good ear) but failed to mention the relationship/emotional context. This omission could have had disastrous results.

Kate also illustrates the importance of the structural context because she lived in a hostel which had not been able to meet her needs for years. The relationship problems could not be sorted out without facing up to this major and intractable problem. Kate gave the impression she did not believe anyone loved her, demanding attention in a way that cut to a minimum the chances of anyone developing a trusting relationship with her. Hostel and day care regimes were obviously not suitable and, despite excellent work by individual workers, her needs had not been met and her behaviour and general attitude to life and to others was slowly deteriorating.

One outstanding volunteer worked with Kate for six months before deciding she could not take it any more – a blow which lowered Kate's self-esteem still further.

The extent of Kate's problem was beyond the efforts of one person and a group consisting of four professionals and three people from local churches decided to try the circles of support approach developed in Canada. This approach faces up to both relationship and structural contexts and is worth describing in detail.

Circles of Support

'Circles of Support' originated in the response of a group of high powered educators in the human services to the total failure of the system in Ontario to meet even the basic needs of an extremely talented but very severely disabled person, Judith Snow. She was leading classes and workshops on political and social aspects of disability in Ontario while living first in an institution, which would not even provide warm meals, and then in a friend's hallway. Her savings were being exhausted paying students to provide care. When all this proved too much she collapsed. One friend took her into her own home and others came up with an emergency plan based on donated time and money. Then:

Two days later when Judith began to talk and regain her strength the five original circle members gathered round and began long range planning. They listened to what Judith wanted and they didn't think it was unreal for her to have a home and a profession such as they had. On large pieces of paper taped to the wall they listed funds available and funds needed. They developed a roster of paid and volunteer attendant care persons. They brainstormed ways to persuade the human-services agencies to respond to Judith's real situation.[3]

Building this package demanded an immense amount of work by a group of able and influential people. At times the project tottered on the edge of failure, but eventually succeeded. Judith now has all the care necessary for her day-to-day needs and leads a satisfying professional life. She is a remarkable person as are the friends who surrounded her. However, this is not the essence of 'circles of support'. This was defined by Peter Dill, one of the original circle: 'He... held the quiet, intuitive belief that five persons (plus Judith) together could mysteriously generate a power much more than each of the five separately. He was right'.[3]

Circles of support have worked effectively for people with learning difficulties. Beth Mount, Pat Beeman and George Ducharme, of Communitas in Connecticut, have developed the approach and describe it as follows: *A circle of support is a group of people who agree to meet on a regular basis to help the person with a disability accomplish certain personal visions or goals. The focus person is unable to reach their goals working alone, so s/he asks a number of people to work with her/him to overcome obstacles and to open doors to new opportunities. The circle members provide support to the focus person and they take action on her/his behalf.*

They add: *Plans tend to become hardened – they lack the capacity to change. If you take the first step towards a dream, the dream will change as you go along. The dream will be changed by reality, but the dream will also change reality.*[4]

They distinguish circles of support from other planning groups:
Building circles is different from other types of individual planning in human services. A circle of support forms and operates totally in the interest of the focus person. The focus person and/or his/her spokesperson determine every aspect of the circle, including membership, setting, image of the future, frequency of meetings, etc. The circle does not 'belong to the system'. The circle is located in, and depends on, local community for its effectiveness.[5]

Kate's situation demanded some radical thinking and action. As mentioned, the small group met to see if they could discover Kate's dream and then try and make it happen.

Circles of support illustrate the principle that it is often sounder if more than one person links with those with learning difficulties. Links that do not depend on a single person reduce individual pressure and allow for such things as holidays. Volunteers, etc. may move, die or give up the link in the same way they terminate other relationships. When a group is involved, the impact of one person leaving is much less.

Circles of support acknowledge the hard graft often necessary when considering the relationship context and the structural context. The circle of support for Kate Briggs was only just starting on the hard graft that would be needed.

The value of past relationships

I have made this point a number of times. Giving attention to past relationships can be highly rewarding.

Sustaining relationships and networks

It is important to know who is in touch with whom. In my research in Dinnington with Rosalind Seyd and Alan Tennant we developed a matrix to describe the work of a community social worker.[6] One category, Network System Consultant, may sound cumbersome but it describes a vital role. Community social work (or, for that matter, community district nursing, health visiting, doctoring etc.) rests on the understanding that the vast bulk of the work is done by ordinary members of the community in the complex of informal care, concern, love and friendship without the involvement of any officials. The community social worker (or similar worker) should enable ordinary people to care, support, etc. as they wish and with less stress. Responsibility is shared, not taken away, so that people may care effectively without assuming improper burdens.

Putting people capable of helping one another in touch (ie. mutual help) is a major contribution. Two families I put in touch included daughters, both in their twenties, who seemed to have similar interests. Both sets of parents, too, seemed to want their daughters to be as independent as possible. There was an extensive network of people with learning difficulties at Hillside. Two key people, John and Philippa Mason, were strong members of the local Anglican church, one source of support and information. Other sources of support included a group run by two social workers and an adult education class. Joyce Goodwin from the local Methodist church attended the adult education cookery class where she helped people with learning difficulties. Three people from the local hostel attended the Methodist church. Joyce Goodwin's husband, Arthur, took people to a luncheon club run by a receptionist from a local general practice. The practice had strong community links, including a local health project with groups and activities possibly appropriate to people with learning difficulties. In the midst of all these contacts and activities, were further possible links, all more likely to succeed because of the existing network.

Relationships and networks are sources of both strength and anguish. Much of the social work input at the Helden club is best described as 'network crises'. Such networks only flourished because they were tended (and even then they sometimes failed).

A major way of enriching the lives of those with learning difficulties is to make their routine varied and interesting. This is implicit in my emphasis on the importance of structure as, for example the benefits to be derived from the structure provided by a proper job. The point is also made strongly by Margaret Flynn: *People whose days are not structured are far more likely to express dissatisfaction with their interpersonal relationships than those in employment (open or sheltered), the ATC, college or voluntary work...People who are occupied during the day fare far better than those who are not.*[7]

Alertness is necessary when altering a routine. Anthony Turner regularly had tea at the staffed group home with Brian Attwell and then went on to his flat (pp.38-39). Brian was keen to invite Anthony for Christmas Day but it was not a Monday and Anthony seemed incapable of coping with this change. He probably wanted it very much but unfortunately nobody was available to ensure he got down to the group home. Something similar happened with John Edwards. A routine was established for him to link up on alternate Sundays with Henry Potts (pp37-38), but when Henry invited him to dinner (instead of after dinner, as usual), he did not come, offering lame excuses when I asked him. I can now see that extra help was needed to cope with, what had seemed to me, slight variations from the routine.

Regular sustaining work is not a luxury: it is essential. *When support personnel 'fade out' they are missed by their clients. Services must question the appropriateness of ceasing to visit people on a regular basis.*[8]

The importance of parents
Parents may be seen as the enemy, blocking progress by being protective and defensive. Linda Ward, after reporting on the wide acceptance of self-advocacy and citizen advocacy, writes: *Empowerment of families and relatives so that they may plan a constructive role in service developments affecting their relatives – rather than the more hostile and negative role into which they are so often cast – is, however, almost unknown in this country.*[9]

Having often coped with unreliable services, parents may well be wary of professionals' latest bright idea. Too often the parents carry the can when things do not work out. Hugh Milson's parents never imagined he could manage an adult education class. The social worker persuaded them he would benefit from a recreation group for people with learning difficulties and a most imaginative class for snooker (raising skills to the level where people are confident enough to join in a game) and cooking. Hugh enjoyed joining in these groups and his parents learnt to trust the social worker – later agreeing that Hugh should attend a literacy class not restricted to people with learning difficulties. Hugh's literacy and numeracy improved but the main gain was his social development. He learnt not to waste time going to the toilet and giggling. His social behaviour became more appropriate. The social workers gained his parents' trust via 'safe' segregated activities, then moved him to more integrated activity with their support. Observing Hugh's greater independence encouraged his parents to look for other ways of fostering it Booth, Simons and Booth's study of people being relocated from hospitals and hostels found: *In our study poor communication between staff and families was a recurrent feature, both before and after the moves... The failure of professionals to recognise the role of families is a recurrent theme running through the interviews.*[10]

Jennifer Morton's parents proved to be effective 'care managers' (pp46-47). Felicity Broadhurst and Hilary Fenton were both helped in setting up their flats through the encouragement of parents who remained an important part of their networks (p36). On the other hand, Freda and Geoffrey Parker and Mavis and Simon Turner were deeply hurt by the way their families rejected them. Families will not necessarily support or help, but every effort should be made to include them until it is proved that this is not in the interests of the people with learning difficulties. If parents are treated as allies they are more likely to be a positive asset.

Addressing the situation as a whole

Parts of the service system can act without regard for other parts and sometimes fail to treat parents as partners. For instance, some day centres ban people from the centres sending them back to, or insisting they remain at, their home or residential unit.

Desmond Slater lived with his widowed mother who worked full-time. Desmond could be awkward. One day he had a violent argument at the day centre and was banned from it without any consultation about how his family could cope. Had his mother taken time off work she could have lost her job so Desmond had to be looked after by his elderly grandmother. There was no notion of partnership here – the day services only considered their own needs. Elsewhere somebody banned from a day unit was despatched back to a residential unit which, like many families, could not cope during the day. Both examples demonstrate a failure to understand the importance of partnership in creating a total structure of care for the person concerned – essential if people with learning difficulties and their friends are to have confidence that the services will be dependable and thus able to give them a sense of security.

Facing up to identity as a disabled person

The cruel dilemma which more able people can face in developing close relationships has already been discussed (pp50-52). These people did not want to associate with others with learning difficulties and aspired to romantic relationships with non-handicapped people. The situation was complicated by the glamorous images people had which owed more to television and advertising than to reality.

Things are very different for those on the margins of learning difficulties compared with those who identify themselves this way. Neither Philip Brindley nor Jason Havering who lived together in the health authority house had any identifiable problem about being seen as having learning difficulties. What was necessary was to work with them and those involved with them to achieve the best integration possible with their respective churches. Bernard Wiles also loved going to church and joined in with a will. Gentle negotiation was needed to dissuade him from joining in anthems and sermons, while congregation and choir accepted he would come in on hymns half a line behind. But this was just a matter of reaching a sensible arrangement. Bernard did not feel uncomfortable standing out in the congregation, notably as a result of his loud voice. He was apparently happy to be accepted as he was and did not feel diminished because, for example, he could not read. Mark Hastings, on the other hand, was extremely sensitive about his inability to read.

Considerations about people on the margins of learning difficulties are likely to involve a sub-culture (a word which may suggest separateness which is not fully justified, but serves to make the point). Something of that sub-culture was visible through those who met at the Oldale Community Centre, the Helden Club, the Victor Gentle group and in the group of men who met to play snooker at the Gateway Club and the networks linked in with them. These segregated groups often formed an introduction to integrated activities. Hugh Milson, for example, started in a segregated adult education class and went into an integrated one. Anthony Turner from the Oldale group found a luncheon club he thought was good value and persuaded Freda and Geoffrey Parker to go. (I was encouraged to go too!). Freda and Geoffrey later went on day trips the lunch club organised.

This sub-culture appeared to provide more able people with a network of relationships which allowed them, in varying degrees, to achieve an identity which helped them live with themselves. Being accepted in this way gave some the confidence to venture into wider, less understanding society. It is interesting that someone as well integrated as Geoff Price found Gateway snooker an important part of his weekly routine.

An integral part of this sub-culture could well be a self-advocacy group. Some are able to make the point, so vital to a sense of wellbeing, that, yes, we are disabled people but we are valued in our own right and deserve to be respected and listened to.

People working with those with learning difficulties should recognise the ways in which sub-cultures support some of the more able, providing them with confidence and bridges into more integrated settings. However, some find this unacceptable. Robert Edgerton in his classic study, The Cloak of Competence, wrote: *Whatever the reasons, self-knowledge of mental retardation was totally unacceptable to these ex-patients. These persons cannot both believe that they are mentally retarded and still maintain their self-esteem. Yet they must maintain their self-esteem. Clearly then passing and denial is vital. This point is critical, for the stigma of mental retardation dominates every feature of the lives of these former patients. Without an understanding of this point, there can be no understanding of their lives.*[11]

This was Stan Rivers' dilemma. He rejected the world of learning difficulties yet needed help, support and, above all, a relationship that gave him the sense of 'belonging and attachment'. Garry Phillips felt very much the same. His social worker described him as one who all his life had been 'done unto' by the services and who wanted to escape from them and the learning difficulties world. But things were changing for Garry. His social worker said he was coming to accept himself as a person with a disability but also as worthwhile. Ken Simons in his self-advocacy book says: *Identity emerged a central issue for all the adults with learning difficulties... The key issue for them is a chance to define themselves rather than have a definition imposed upon them.*[12]

This seemed to be what Garry was managing to do. Although he had rejected most services, he was happy to call in to a small local day centre where he had a particular role – taking the post to the social services department headquarters. This made him feel valued. As Ken Simons reports of self-advocates: *Helping others was a central issue for self-advocates. The opportunity to help others is one of the few chances that people have to take on valued roles; it provides status.*

He points out how a sense of 'belonging', often referred to in this book, influenced a 'positive sense of self'. *For some self-advocates (mainly members of the Avon People First) the group became a very significant part of their lives.'You feel you belong to something ...being noticed. It makes living worth while.'*[13]

There remains the original central issue. What happens to people who do not want to belong to groups with learning difficulties, even self-advocacy groups? Garry's response was significant. He did not appear to have a close relationship with anyone but had cultivated a range of comparatively superficial relationships with non-disabled people through visits to the pub and to certain stalls in the town market. Though limited, it allowed Garry to define his identity on his own terms. Ken Simons says this is a key way in which people with learning difficulties are able to acknowledge their limitations: *Such acknowledgements as 'I couldn't cope on my own,' or 'I want some help,' were made both by people who had accepted the idea of having a learning difficulty and by those who felt it did not apply to them. However, there is a critical rider to be added. If asked directly if they found anything difficult many would initially say no. The acknowledgement of limitation generally came in other contexts; the self-advocates would generally make such confidences only on their terms.*[13]

This ambiguity was caught nicely at a conference for people with learning difficulties. They wanted bus passes but did not want to be identified as having learning difficulties. They eventually saw the contradiction and laughed about it.

Clearly there is no simple solution to this complex issue. Just how deeply the issues lie in our society is shown by Marcia Rioux: *The implication is that we all have the benefits of citizenship, not as beggars but as persons entitled to them.*

Human dignity, community, protection of rights and equality have to be substituted for classification (labelling), segregation, and the obligation of those with mental handicaps to prove themselves. In the process, the notion of noblesse oblige will have to be replaced. We must come to see the issue not in terms of what 'we' ought to do for 'them' but what we ought to do for ourselves. We must move the agenda from charity to rights; from best interests to choice; from disempowerment to empowerment; from professional control to self-advocate control; from cost-effectiveness to output-effectiveness; from fixing a weakness (rehabilitation) to developing a strength; from expedient categorisation to individual need; and from service to support.[14]

But in the meantime the self-advocacy movement is breaking important ground in developing the self-confidence and self-esteem of people with learning difficulties.

Self-advocacy is really important in people's lives – until I learnt self-advocacy skills, I didn't really see myself as a person. With all the labels people put on you, you don't have the confidence. Self-advocacy is seeing yourself as a person.[15]

Self-advocacy is not a route everyone will follow but it should have important consequences for the sense of self worth of all people with learning difficulties.

Segregation and integration
The motive behind this project was the need to work for real integration and to accommodate people leaving hostels and hospitals in the areas where they had been living. It seems unnecessary to argue that this is desirable; it is a right of citizenship, as Marcia Rioux argues. However, integration is a means, not an end. The ultimate question is not 'Is this person well integrated into the community?' but 'Is this person happy?'

If the priority of sustaining and developing sound relationships is accepted, it is then much easier to appreciate that this may involve segregated groups. The Helden club is a good example. Both it and the Oldale group often helped people move on to integrated activities.

But a segregated group is not justified just because it facilitates the move to integration, desirable though this is. Segregation may help develop fulfilling relationships which are valuable in their own right. We have seen how important such relationships can be in achieving a sense of 'belonging and attachment'.

Of course it is vital to avoid anything that smacks of 'they like their own kind' and to insist that the aim is to create maximum real choice, especially in relationships, choice that includes the possibility of close and intimate relationships with those who are not disabled as well as those with learning difficulties. Refusal to accept this devalues those involved and suggests they are not worthy of relationships.

I have emphasised the need to enable people to re-establish or retain existing relationships, often with others with learning difficulties. But this must not detract from the value of overcoming the 'friendship barrier' and making friends with non-disabled people. This may well include intimate relationships.

Booth and Booth looked at parental experiences of people with learning difficulties. Eleven couples lived together. Both partners of four couples had learning difficulties, while only one partner in each of the other seven had. Two other couples were not living together. In one both partners had learning difficulties, in the other only one.[16] People with learning difficulties need encouragment and support in developing relationships with people without disabilities. Breaking out of the learning difficulties mould may be painful but it is important, wherever possible, for all our sakes.

Ann Shearer wrote about the Islington adult education Links scheme which mixes volunteers and those with learning difficulties to take advantage of evening classes. Her conclusion is a good way of finishing this chapter:

'I'm sorry', a Links student said politely but firmly to her volunteer in their class, 'but you just don't do it that way'. She was right, too. For Jacquie Billis the exchange conveyed the essence of what Links is trying to achieve. The student had recognised her own ability - and found the confidence to express that. The volunteer was set to think about how often people with learning disabilities feel able to correct others when they are wrong, and so about wider issues of relationships between the 'able' and the 'disabled' world. Links is about integration that is a two-way process of learning.[17]

References

1. Grant, G., Ramcharan, P. and McGrath, M. (1993) Living in the Community: Views of three people with a learning disability, Centre for Social Policy Research and Development, University of Wales, Bangor, LL57 2DG.
This quotation includes the following refererences:
(a) Dunst, C.J., Trivette, C.M., Gordon, N.J. and Pletcher, L.L.(1989) Building and mobilizing informal family support networks. In: Singer, G.H.S. and Irwin, L.K. (eds) Support for Caregiving Families: Enabling Positive Adaption to Disability. Baltimore: Paul H. Brookes.
b) Edgerton, R.B. (ed) (1984) Lives in Process: Mildly Retarded Adults in a Large City, Washington: AAMD.
(c) Grant, G., McGrath, M. and Ramcharan, P. (1993) How families and informal supporters appraise service quality. Submitted to International Journal of Disability, Development and Education.
2. Brechin, A. and Swain, (1982) Unit 8 Mental Handicap and Integration, The Handicapped Person in the Community, Milton Keynes: Open University Press, p.63.
3. Perske, R. (1988) Circles of Friends, Nashville, USA: Abingdon Press, p.17.
4. Mount, B., Beeman, P. and Ducharme, G., What are we learning about Circles of Support?, Communitas Inc., Manchester, Connecticut, USA, p.3.
5. Ibid. p.18.
6. Bayley, M., Seyd, R. and Tennant, A. (1989) Local Health and Welfare: A study of the Dinnington Project, Aldershot: Gower, p.121.
7. Flynn, M.C. (1989) Independent Living for Adults with Mental Handicap: A Place of My Own, London: Cassell, p.120.
8. Ibid. p.120.
9. Ward, L. (1989) For better, for worse, Making Connections (eds Brechin, A. and Walmesley, J.) London: Hodder & Stoughton, p.196.
10. Booth, T., Simons, K. and Booth, W. (1990) Outward Bound: Relocation and Community Care for People with Learning Difficulties, Milton Keynes: Open University Press, pp.148 and 150.
11. Edgerton, Robert B. (1971) The Cloak of Competence, University of California Press, pp.207f.
12. Simons, K. (1992) Sticking up for yourself: self advocacy and people with learning difficulties, Joseph Rowntree Foundation/Community Care, p.75.
13. Ibid. p.26.
14. Rioux, M.H. (1992-93) The Contradiction of Kindness; The Clarity of Justice, in Entourage, Vol.7., No.4., Winter 1992-93, p.22.
15. Flynn, M. and Ward., L. (1991) We can change the Future: Self and Citizen Advocacy, Prospects for People with Learning Difficulties (eds Segal, S.S. and Varma, V.P.) London: David Fulton Publishers, p.129f.
16. Booth, T. and Booth, W. (1994) Parenting under Pressure: Mothers and Fathers with Learning Difficulties, Buckingham: Open University Press, p.4.
17. Shearer, A. (1986) Building Community, London: Campaign for People with Mental Handicaps and King's Fund Publishing.

Chapter IX
A befriending scheme

I need a friendship: I wish I had a companion, a boy I could have as a companion, that I could go out with and chat to. I have nobody and it hurts me. I'd like someone to go around with, like girls in the club. They have their own friends and they go around with each other. (Republic of Ireland)

In outlining the need to break through the friendship barrier (Chapter I) I found I had an inadequate theoretical framework. My aim has been to improve on this, showing how relationships, structures and sustaining fit together.

Friendship schemes do have a part to play but they require a better chance of success. This chapter shows what was learnt during the project about befriending. It needs to be taken in context with Chapters IV - VII (a range of possible entry points) and Chapter VIII (some general principles).

Discovering a person's interests
My favourite example remains Michael Preston's simple expression of priorities. Asked what he liked, he replied, "Sitting next to June". Few people sort things out as clearly as this.

My initial interviews sought to find out what the person with learning difficulties could and could not do, the emphasis being on what they liked to do. Often parents or a carer were present and it was difficult to persuade interviewees who could speak to speak for themselves. Apart from an apparent lack of confidence in the presence of strangers, many people's experience was so limited that they had had little opportunity to discover the possibilities. This posed some interesting problems; for example, Freda Parker lived with her husband in a very pleasant flat and revealed she liked cleaning, polishing and keeping her flat nice and tidy. This could have been the result of limited experience, with hostel domestic staff as her only role models. Such limitations must be acknowledged but it is also important to take what people say seriously. Freda and her husband, Geoffrey, attended an excellent further education class which provided a wide range of leisure activities, so it seemed fair to assume that Freda's interest in cleaning was a positive choice, not just an inability to think of anything else. In view of this I found a simple cleaning job for Freda but she did not want to do it! Perhaps it was because she was not very well at the time and perhaps because she needed more support than I could give.

Philip Brindley, who lived with Jason Havering in a house owned and run by the health authority, posed the same problem in a different way. Although he could not speak, his behaviour made one thing clear – apart from liking music, he enjoyed sitting down and doing nothing. When do you say 'This is his choice' since this could become an excuse for not encouraging Philip to expect more from life. The temptation to accept Philip's apathy was strong but other factors suggested it was worthwhile persisting.

Achieving a balance between giving the person with learning difficulties a chance to speak and also drawing on the insights of parents was not always easy. It was distressing talking to an adult with learning difficulties while parents told me all the things he or she could not do. I developed simple strategies like asking questions while out on a walk with the person with learning difficulties. Sometimes I had to spend time gaining the parents' trust and encouraging them to recognise their offspring's competence. Even if parents do not display all the attitudes professionals deem desirable, they still need to be regarded as allies.

Some parents were careful not to speak for their son or daughter if at all possible. Others, as expected, supplied valuable insights into their interests. It was Felicity Broadhurst's parents who mentioned the fascinating group of friends centred round Victor Gentle (p55).

Perhaps the most encouraging feature of this aspect of the project was the sympathetic and perceptive insights of many people working with people with learning difficulties. Key workers in day centres often appeared to know – more than anyone else – what would improve the lives of those for whom they were responsible, and I was struck by the accuracy of their suggestions. Key workers mentioned Michael Preston's close relationship with June Heston and Christopher Johnson's relationship with Mary Cartwright. The greatest insight into Anthony Turner's mercurial character came from his key worker.

An obvious but important point is that it is vital to tap all sources of information. There is no way a worker like myself could match the knowledge and experience of those who had worked with people with learning difficulties, perhaps for years. External insights should always acknowledge the experience of parents, family, social, residential or day care worker or home helps. A profound, though not uncritical, respect should be extended to those who know the person well, as well as to the person.

What's available in the wider community

Discovering this was a major, time-consuming job. It involved establishing a network of contacts with statutory, voluntary and informal bodies to achieve sensitive and satisfactory links offering real choice. People who knew those with learning difficulties were also approached about activities in the locality. Local day centres which were replacing the centralised centres made a useful start through the discovery of luncheon clubs where people could both dine and help in a staff role. Directing people to appropriate further education classes was also beneficial.

Identifying rambling clubs was not enough: I needed those which would take in a person with learning difficulties. Similarly with churches: I needed to enlist the goodwill of the priest or minister and know there were people at the church who would make the person with learning difficulties welcome. There are good models. The Mencap Pathway scheme and the Sheffield Health Authority Intowork project devote time, energy and resources to establishing links with potential employers, preparing the employees (the people with learning difficulties) for the work and supporting them and the employers for as long as necessary. I found that similar commitment was needed to establish appropriate links in the community. The time needed to establish and maintain such a network of contacts is often underestimated. It was a great disadvantage that I did not have a proper base in the area.

Also, the project was in some ways too small. Concentrating on a limited number of people had its advantages but matching up people's interests demands as big a 'bank' as possible. For example, when I was looking for an aeroplane enthusiasts' club, I had no luck but I did find, as I recounted above, an obliging woman who was prepared to take people up in her light aircraft. This was no good for the person who wanted an aeroplane enthusiasts' club because he suffered from travel sickness but it helped Geoffrey Parker who was able to take it up. It helped that I was in touch with a wide 'bank' of people.

Senior staff in one of the hostels gave me the names of two retired staff members who they thought might be interested in working as volunteers with people with learning difficulties. After a long conversation with one of them, Nancy Evans, it was evident she was interested in developing the relationships she had had with some of the people in the hostel over the previous 17 years. She was already going down to the hostel regularly to see people but, eventually, we agreed she should contact one old man, Harry Grey, whom she knew well and liked. He had moved out of the hostel but was not very well. Subsequently, she went with him to the hostel where he used to live and to the pub he liked to frequent, activities that looked like making the last years of his life significantly happier.

Note what was necessary to make this link :
• Recognition of the potential contribution of retired members of staff from the hostel.
• A senior member of staff in the hostel who was prepared to make some suggestions.
• Awareness of the need to build on existing strengths of the retired staff member and on what she would be happy with, rather than trying to persuade her to do something else.
• A reasonably wide knowledge of people with learning difficulties in the area and their needs.
• Time and ability to support and encourage the relationship.

In this case my contact with both people concerned was minimal. It was not so much that I knew them as that I knew who knew them and knew who could be trusted – perhaps the clearest example of working as a broker.

That principle could usefully be developed. In my case I might have benefited from a much wider range of contacts. This raises questions about being part of a team which I consider in the next chapter.

Convincing service systems that friendship matters

Friendships for people with learning difficulties often appear to count for little in the estimation of those who control their lives. In some cases administrative neatness seemed to count for more. Statutory workers, parents and whoever, need to be made aware of the importance of friendship in order that their organisations act accordingly: ie. that they see relationships as primary. It may seem odd that this point has to be made with the social services but such organisations can become so rigid they cannot respond to the untidiness of individual need.

The policy implications of this are considered in the next chapter.

Enabling people and organisations to fulfil their proper functions

As the project progressed I became aware that although the core of the project – ie. fostering friendship – is close to what makes life worthwhile for all of us, it does not necessarily appear on the official agenda of the formal services. This tends to distort organisations concerned with people with learning difficulties. For example, advocacy should be able to concentrate on advocacy. But because no organisation takes friendship needs sufficiently seriously, the advocacy office often deals with a need for friendship dressed up as a need for advocacy.

And, in providing residential care, the statutory services may well be bypassing needs for friendship because it is an issue they are not equipped to grapple with. This was certainly true at the house run by the health authority where Philip Brindley and James Havering lived. The staff had simply not been trained to take account of it. Once encouraged, they responded readily. However, to the best of my knowledge they initiated no new local contacts once I stopped working with them.

Helping organisations establish deeper friendships

Deeper relationships are needed wherever the contact is only superficial and its full potential is not being realised. This was the situation when Jason Havering attended the Roman Catholic church with members of staff from the house where he was living. It required persistent encouragement from me for over a year before Jason's relationship with Mrs Carter and her family was established (p74). Similar exploration, work and encouragement helped develop deeper friendships from Philip Brindley's church attendance (pp71-72) and James Pearson's association with the snooker club (p48).

There seems to be better recognition of this sort of work in Canada. In an article, The Community Experience for a Few Albertans Who Have Left Institutions, Catherine Duchesne writes: *Three years ago, after involvement in many advocacy campaigns, demonstration projects, individual sponsorships and community education events, the leaders of this group understood that technological and systematic change is not enough. The world of services, within the institution and the community, cannot replace what most people who live with a disability lack:*

*a sense of belonging, acceptance, personal relationships and friend-
ship. It was time to leave the service system to others and to turn their
attention to creating opportunities for individual adults to participate in
community life.*

*Personal Communities' activities now focus on guiding isolated indi-
vidual adults into the hub of community life. This is through membership of an association or group that meets regularly to pursue an interest common to the members. This is an intentional effort to enmesh
persons with disabilities (representing a variety and complexity of
needs) with community life. The Personal Communities worker uses
approaches that support both the individual and the association. Each
individual benefits by experiencing membership, belonging and greater
self-esteem and by gaining opportunities to develop personal relationships. The community association or group is strengthened by having
a greater capacity to welcome and include. Further, the association
becomes a model for other groups and individual members whose
sphere of influence extends into the greater community...*

*(However) most communities require support for interpreting the needs
of the individual, and need encouragement to be more inclusive.*[1]

We need to concentrate on people's need for friendship because our
society has become curiously distorted. Often people with learning
difficulties suffer disproportionately from society's defects, and serious re-learning is needed about enabling people to become fully human. Experiences in residential communities such as L'Arche may
provide guidance. Here, relationships are accepted as being of prime
importance and, when they are working well, gives those living there a
valued role in which they can feel secure.

Working with professionals and other paid workers
One satisfactory example of professional and volunteer collaboration
occurred when Philip Brindley's reluctance to leave events was overcome (pp71-72). This was not a case of a professional passing on
expertise to a volunteer but rather an alert professional recognising
the significance of a volunteer's success elsewhere. A major aspect of
the project approach is the development and fostering of this sort of
trusting relationship between paid workers and volunteers.

The importance of back-up
When Philip refused to leave the Gilbert and Sullivan rehearsals, the

volunteer delivering him and taking him back said, very reasonably, she could not cope with this at the end of a busy day. As a result he could only attend when there were two staff on in the evening and transport was available.

When we discovered the significance of taking off Philip's coat I re-contacted the volunteer but she was still reluctant. One reason was that if anything went wrong (eg. not getting Philip's coat off in time) she could not be sure help would be readily available since there was of-ten only one staff member on duty at the house. Back-up is vital and no volunteer should be denied it or left in the dark about it. In this project the main back-up came from members of staff at day centres (the new local day centres were particularly good in this respect), so-cial workers and residential staff. However, if befriending is to be de-veloped, more back-up will be needed. Those who need friends most are those who may pose problems. If members of the public are in-volved they need to know help will be quickly available. Cell phones are an effective aid but an added expense. However, if service sys-tems are serious about wanting to involve the public in caring for, and supporting, disadvantaged people, such support is essential.

The role of the worker
Who is the worker? For the moment I am assuming he or she is a social worker or community nurse based simply on the situations I encountered in this project. I would expect the worker to adopt the methods outlined in the previous chapter, especially with regard to the priority of relationships.

However, there is one particular role a worker needs to play in support of a befriending scheme, that is both to coordinate and to accept re-sponsibility. In the imaginative arrangement by which people from the Helden club looked after one another (p64) the social worker arranged, coordinated and was responsible for them.

In this project it was often difficult to find a worker who took responsi-bility. Sometimes I took it but this was unsatisfactory as my job was only temporary. At other times, because no worker bore responsibility for the case and the person involved lived with parents, the burden fell on the parents.

The issue of responsibility raises the importance of continuity. The worker or, more accurately, the agency has a continuing responsibility.

Yet staff turnover complicates this. It is said that one couple became so fed up with briefing yet another social worker about their daughter they made a tape recording.

If nothing else this should encourage workers to support those who offer more continuity than they can. These include parents, friends from mental handicap hospitals, long-standing key workers at day centres, retired members of staff from hostels who remain in touch, or family members who are terrified at being landed with a responsibility with which they cannot cope.

The relationship to advocacy

The complementary roles of advocacy and meeting friendship needs have already been discussed in this chapter. Although distinct, the roles are closely related and it seems likely more people will be able to offer friendship than would wish to act as an advocate. Any scheme for developing friendship would benefit from a separate advocacy body working in the same area.

Failures

There were many failures. A weekly tea dance with live thirties and forties music for old people and people with learning difficulties (thought up in collaboration with a worker at the local day centre) seemed a good idea but did not work. Nor did encouraging the day centre staff to try circle dancing, even though I think the staff at least enjoyed learning how to do it.

Links failed for a variety of reasons: illness, anxiety, unexplained dropouts. Experience indicates this is inevitable and indeed natural. Links of friendship must be links that are freely made. In setting up a link I emphasised that either side always had the right to opt out if they were not happy. Giving people with learning difficulties more choice inevitably means some 'failures'.

I was particularly disappointed that a scheme for recruiting volunteers through a local general practice did not work. Three people did offer help but, for various reasons, none was a success. Given more time and a larger pool of people with learning difficulties, it might have been possible to establish some links. One problem was that when people visit the doctor they are normally in need and this may not be a good time to approach them. Despite the disappointments I believe the scheme has potential as a means of recruiting people from the locality.

Time
A maddening aspect was that as the three-year project drew to an end more people emerged wanting to be involved. It takes a long time for a scheme like this to take hold.

Practical details
Relevant literature on setting up a formal friendship scheme is given in Appendix A.

Where befriending may be especially important
Stan Rivers, whose situation haunts this book, desperately needed a friend. Being that friend would be immensely demanding emotionally. Mark Hastings longed for a sexual partner, so did Arthur Needles, so did Garry Phillips. Kate Briggs needed an accepting, affirming place to live and the relationships to go with it. It is appropriate that this chapter should end by asking how far the services are genuinely user-oriented. Following implementation of the NHS and Community Care Act the talk was about how services would focus on user needs and how carers' needs would receive real attention. Too many examples here show this was not the case. The failure of the services over the years to respond to the real needs of Kate Briggs is particularly eloquent (p59).

But imaginative responses to needs have been made, a good example being the package put together for Matthew Exton (pp52-54) after his mother died. Good ideas and imaginative practices exist; the problem is finding ways of enabling them to percolate, especially to managers. The solution is not (another!) re-organisation but a style of management and an organisational culture which encourages good ideas to rise up as well as management's instructions to pass down. Worker supervision should be an opportunity for ideas to pass up the line and for managers to identify ways in which the system is thwarting user interests rather than simply a means of telling workers about the administrative arrangements into which they must fit.

No-one is going to pretend that this is easy in a large accountable organisation operating in a harsh economic and political climate. But there are still many ways of being creative with, and on behalf of, people with learning difficulties. The fundamental commitment needed is to accept the priority of relationships and the creation of structures which support them. This is far more challenging than might be expected. The final chapter looks at ways in which policy may need to develop to make this a reality.

References
1. Duchesne, C. (1992) The Community Experience for a Few Albertans Who Have Left Institutions, *Entourage*, Vol. 17, No.2, Summer 1992, pp.7 and 8.

Chapter X
Policy implications

One day, I remember talking to a man in my ward who had been in hospital for 39 years. I remember thinking that life wouldn't be worth much if the same happened to me. I began to think about a flat of my own, a job, a girl friend, how I wanted those things for myself. (Robert: Dunfermline)

Befriending schemes have their place but the basic need is for service systems in which relationships are seen as central and there are appropriate structures to support them. A system in which Michael Preston and June Haston would have transport to meet regularly (pp39-41). And, should their relationship develop to the point where they wanted to live together, the support for this would be forthcoming, as for Martin and Jenny Fry (pp60-61).

Is such support unrealistic at a time when all services are under financial pressure and when it is difficult to persuade authorities to take a long term view?

I have two reasons for arguing that investment in relationships would be sound. First, anticipate what will happen when Michael's mother dies. Making proper provision for Michael and June now would not be cheap but it would forestall emergency action and would probably cost less in the long run. Proper provision for Kate Briggs now would be less expensive than waiting till she explodes in spectacular fashion and then needs an out-of-authority placement.

Second, and more important, such investment stands a better chance of enabling people to lead more complete and satisfying lives. Here the arguments are: the satisfaction on Philip Brindley's face when he saw Miss Polkington, Jason Havering's jump after he received communion, Arthur Needles' response to a visit by his splendid volunteer, the mutual pleasure generated when Bruce Mander looked after Hilda Hessing for a few days, the delight in each other's company experienced by Michael and June. If this approach is simply romantic, then romantic is what we must be. If community living is to be more than a political slogan, we must find means of honouring, encouraging and supporting relationships which make people alive.

We are not starting from scratch and there are some important and encouraging clues.

The matrix as a check

I hesitate to suggest more forms but the matrix on page 33 could help check whether the needs for particular relationships are being met. The necessary information fits on to a sheet of A4; (see Appendix B for examples: the precariousness of Christopher Johnson's situation contrasted with John and Philippa Mason's much richer environment). One of its values is that the matrix encourages people to ask the important questions.

The matrix might be developed by including not just assets but also drawbacks. Parents might supply a sense of 'belonging and attachment', while undermining their offspring by putting him or her down (a drawback under 'reassurance of worth').

Networking

Support groups and networks (Chapter VI) are probably the richest source of relationships. Local day centres also proved to be potential focal points for networks.

Hostel staff had similar opportunities although tight staffing levels limited them even more than day care workers. Some home care aides played significant roles in providing relationships (Matthew Exton, pp52-54) and in enabling the development of further relationships (John Edwards, pp37-38). Organisations, mostly churches, can help meet the need for some relationships perhaps at quite a profound level. The importance of picking up on old friendships has also been demonstrated.

What sort of worker?

What sort of worker can consistently adopt the necessary approaches? Who will have the time to establish links with community organisations and support them continuously? Who will call together people who do not usually meet in order to take into account the whole life of a person in need? Who will spend time and energy to ensure Arthur Needles gets to the painting and drawing adult education class now that his mother's arthritis is so bad? Who will bully the system until Arthur is given the road crossing training he needs to get there by himself?

Coordinating these differing responsibilities is likely to fall to a social worker. The task of contacting community organisations and winkling out support will probably occupy a community worker. Those most regularly in touch are parents, residential care staff, day care staff and domiciliary care staff.

It is difficult to imagine effective action being taken without at least one person taking on the specific job of developing this way of working. That said, one person alone would almost certainly be ground down by the system.

A locally based health and welfare model would provide the most appropriate organisational base[1]; unfortunately, current practice seems to be moving in the opposite direction. Essentially, locally based teams of workers from different disciplines and agencies interweave their help and resources with the care, competence and concern of family, friends, neighbours and local organisations. Emphasis is on such basic courtesies as local workers keeping in touch with clients, families and one another, and passing on relevant information.

In one area of the town, outside the project, a pattern of care – or perhaps an infra-structure of support – started to develop and showed great promise. It had some features in common with the Dinnington project. The housing stock was especially suitable for people with learning difficulties who were moving out of residential care because (a) there were a lot of single flats, and (b) turnover was quite rapid.

Unfortunately, the original highly effective family aide service (ie. home help type workers providing practical and moral support) was subsequently much reduced. A core of people knew one another through the family aide service and some had lived in the same hostel. When the latter closed down, people moved into nearby homes and flats. Others with learning difficulties wanted to move into the area because they knew support was available. When workers realised how isolated many of the people moving in were, they found ways of enabling them to make links, notably through the creation of the Helden Club. More moved in because they had friends there and because they sensed opportunities to develop friendships. Since phones and cars were rare, nearness was essential if networks were to be sustained.

Specialist family aide support was vital to the system and most if not all people with learning difficulties in a limited local area were visited. Thus the family aide linked people and became an important line of communication. This was particularly effective because the network enabling role was linked to home care maintenance, a role which was readily acceptable and obviously required regular contact. Family aides have another important role: they pass on gossip and other useful information. Social worker back-up was vital as was the network supported and encouraged by the Helden Club.

If a sense of community for people with learning difficuties can be created in a defined area with suitable housing this may lead to many of the advantages available in some residential communities but at much lower cost and in a more integrated way.

Here, then, is the beginnings of a pattern based on the priority of relationships. In the structures created, people receive the support they need to make their own relationships, similar in some ways to those made through the workplace.

The answer to 'What sort of worker?' is one who, as well as understanding the approach, is part of a team. Key team members will often be low paid domiciliary care staff whose contribution is frequently underestimated. This also raises questions about the poor pay they receive.

The impact of the NHS and Community Care Act (1990)
Much of this chapter has been about teamwork, networking, supporting community organisations. It is concerned with people's social environment – ie. work unattributable directly to the needs of any individual.

Such work may be threatened if the NHS and Community Care Act is implemented in too narrow a way. The Act focuses on the individual and on putting together an individual care package. If contracted-out services extend to fieldwork, it is possible to imagine that the only paid services will be those explicitly related to an individual's needs. This has not happened at the time of writing (May 1994) but remains a possibility.

If we are going to take seriously the importance of enabling people with learning difficulties to develop a full range of relationships, then it will be vital to ensure that the service system is able to sustain, support and encourage wider social networks.

Beyond that, the challenge will be to develop packages which recognise the priority of relationships and the need to provide the structures and support to sustain them. Some of these issues are considered in the next section.

Creating a life-enhancing environment

There should not be an uncritical assumption that our goal should be maximum independence; rather it should be the creation of a life-enhancing environment. Brechin and Swain give a good example: *To be human is not simply a question of being able to carry out certain functions but, more importantly, it also involves taking part in the life of society, making one's own choices and, if necessary, making one's own mistakes. A paralysed person, therefore, may resist travelling to church independently in an Invacar (which can carry no passengers) and prefer to be pushed by a helper, being lifted up kerbs and steps on the way, because the social contact this involves is construed as more important than independent movement from one place to another.*

They go on: *What we are arguing here is that it is uncovering the person's intentions which sets the criterion for deciding whether an aid is likely to be appropriate for the achievement of a particular goal... All too often functions such as walking or dressing are taken as goals in themselves and much effort is spent in trying to achieve these ends, sometimes to the exclusion of the actual, but non-conscious, purpose of that function... For example, the mentally handicapped person, lacking social skills, may express an interest in football and then be aided to follow this interest. Here, the specific social interest would be taken as the focus for deciding the appropriate solution and this could range from training in particular skills (such as using public transport, buying a ticket and so on), to providing human aid to take the person to the match.*[2]

One way of implementing this approach can be seen in the package developed for Martin and Jenny Fry (pp60-61). Much of their life together had been disrupted by their inability to cope with money. During ten hours a week of home care, the carer, among other things, enabled them to keep their money under control, a major factor in stabilising their relationship. (The worker was also good at smoothing out other problems). Although it seemed likely Martin and Jenny would always need that help, it is unhelpful to label a situation as a failure if people are not pushed to greater and greater independence. Instead, continuing help should be seen as an appropriate aid for living. It is difficult to say what level of help is appropriate and what is over-protection, denying the dignity of risk. Such dilemmas arise, for instance, in keeping a flat clean, ensuring medication is taken, help with shopping, cooking or diet, sorting out relationships, reading letters aloud, paying bills and making sure people get away on holiday. As Flynn and Hirst say: 'Ordinary lives often require extraordinary supports'.[3]

Provided professionals recognise the dignity and value of people with learning difficulties and work to find ways in which they can express themselves as valued, loved and loving individuals, then the danger of getting hung up over words like 'independence' is reduced. Concentrating on enabling people to develop relationships reduces the chance of being patronising and over-protective.

Thus if help with money enriches a relationship and lack of such help sours it, there is every reason to regard this as an appropriate aid which promotes appropriate interdependence. It empowers rather than diminishes. One view suggests that people with walking problems should struggle on as long as they can to keep on their feet. However, in some instances it is far better to accept a wheelchair and conserve energy for more creative and satisfying activities.

Having enough money and living without victimisation are key needs, as Margaret Flynn explains. Martin and Jenny did quite well out of the benefit system and were reasonably comfortable but Anthony Turner was quite hard-pressed. As a result he was mean with money and worried about the cost of giving someone a cup of tea. Lack of money affected his social relationships. It is not that we give people with learning difficulties appropriate help with money, rather we shackle them with inappropriate poverty.

Mobility is a related issue. Despite concessionary fares, people with learning difficulties have problems in travelling around and this too affects their relationships. Michael Preston and June Heston could not travel independently and when they stopped attending the same training centre they were unable to keep in touch. Here, empowerment means being able to travel. Solving this problem will always be fairly expensive but it must be faced if supporting relationships is to be a part of care in the community.

If we respond to the needs of people with learning difficulties by helping them develop relationships (with appropriate structures) and providing appropriate aids to maintain those relationships, we have a good chance of remaining on course.

Peter Kinsella's book, Supported Living: A New Paradigm[4], adopts a similar approach. Supported living has a gentleness and sensitivity which does not always characterise new thinking about improving the lives of people with learning difficulties. It focuses absolutely on what they want, not on what others think they ought to want, as in what he says about size of household: *Supported living is not about size, nor about having an optimal number of people living together. It is about choosing who you live with – if that is with another three people, so be it.*[5]

Not surprisingly there is a firm emphasis on listening: *Regardless of the specifics of the support, the people in providing this support must develop new ways of truly listening to people with learning disabilities.*[6]

Parallel with that, Kinsella sees that: *Decisions cannot be made by remote bureaucracies but by people who are closest to the individual.*[7]

There is a focus on relationships and the support they need: *The starting point is to build on a person's existing relationships and connections. Paid help is only used when natural and informal supports are not available. Paid supporters work to develop a person's social network alongside their other activities.*

Supported living is... a process to enable people with learning disabilities to be included in their communities and be fully and actively involved in them. The aim of furnishing services and supports to a programme participant is to assist that individual to take command of his or her life while building critical and durable relationships with other individuals.[8]

Kinsella also emphasises the importance of financial security, flexible support and, above all, relationships: *For people with learning disabilities, Supported Living is about financial security: having enough money for a decent standard of living, having control over that money and deciding what to spend it on. It means having flexible and dynamic supports that are tailored to each person's situation and which change as their needs and expectations change. It is about having comprehensive supports (from paid and unpaid people) which are available when you want and need them. Supported Living means being accepted for who you are and what you are - it means understanding the person and their disability and what it means to them.*

Supported Living is the natural seeking out and making use of the capacity and potential of communities and people's social networks. This includes accessing the range of ordinary housing stock available to the rest of the population. Supported Living is about people with disabilities retaining power and control over their own lives and being in control of their own destiny. It is about leadership, with the leadership coming from people with disabilities.

Supported Living is about full inclusion and full participation in the communities in which people live. It is about mutual support and interdependence – giving and receiving. In Supported Living, the relationship between people with disabilities and their supports is one of reciprocity, based on personal relationships and commitment. Supported Living is about living with people and having people around you who love you and care about you.[9]

In short, supported living is about creating a life-enhancing environment.

Work
Work may:
• Provide meaningful occupation.
• Build self-esteem and thus affect the way people behave.
• Facilitate integration and the establishment of friendships.
• Provide more money.

Meaningful occupation includes work in training centres as well as work outside. Some people missed the industrial work that used to be done in the training centres. Brian Attwell, for instance, felt he was doing something real even though he was not receiving a proper wage. He found recreational activities unfulfilling. A Mencap study of day care found a similar situation: *Now all of a sudden... there was a... parents' meeting, and we were told the unit was leaving the centre, that it would be phased out over two years... we thought it was a damn good thing. Seven weeks later the unit was taken out of the centre – everything. That's why they are all sitting round on their backsides.* (Parent, Midlands)[10]

However valuable day-centre work may be and however much it may generate a sense of self-esteem, the almost universal finding is that most people would prefer a proper job with real wages. An independent survey of students' views at Swallow Street Centre in Kirklees found that, given a choice, 62 per cent of students interviewed would prefer a proper job with real wages.[11]

Despite the recession much progress has been made in finding jobs for people with learning difficulties. The Real Jobs Programme has shown what is possible. Barry Connolly has learning difficulties and is a full-time kitchen porter at Leicester Forest Moat House Hotel. He said: *My life has changed because of my work. I feel proud because I can hold down a job and do it as well as anyone else. My workmates respect me and they have also become my friends. My home is no longer a prison but somewhere I go and relax.*[12]

A study of seven people in supported employment shows how a job can enhance the quality of life and provide the opportunity for at least a degree of integration with non-disabled people. Alison Westheimer comments: *Community presence doesn't necessarily equal community participation and the job trainer and others will need to adopt a pro-active approach to ensure that the person is not missing out on opportunities for social contact.*[13]

The extent to which the seven people made friends through their work varied considerably, but for some it was very successful.

Supported employment clearly has a lot to offer. A tentative assessment suggests: *That the running costs of most supported employment services are comparable with those of more traditional day services.*[14] However, only about 2,000 people are employed compared with nearly 70,000 at adult training centres.

Supported employment recommends that people are placed separately from others with learning difficulties, while being supported by a job coach. Good results are possible but whether the practice is ideal for everyone is open to question. In some cases co-operative groups which mix those with learning disabilities and non-disabled people might be better.

Antur Waunfawr (The Waunfawr Venture), set in quite a small village near Caernarfon in North Wales, aims to integrate a group of people with learning difficulties into the village community. It has proved that group work can be fulfilling and can lead to worthwhile integration. The work involves transforming derelict cottages into living accommodation and a shop; developing adjacent land for horticultural/agricultural/animal husbandry purposes; developing a small industries unit and community projects; selling produce and wares generated through the shop. The number involved rose to ten men and four women with learning difficulties plus, for part of the time, six local unemployed people covered by the Community Programme Scheme.The scheme administrator, Hywel Vaughan Evans, writes: *The change in the Antur Waunfawr workers came about, therefore, because of meaningful work, no experience of failure, and a chance to be like other people in a calculated risk environment. Nine of them now handle strimmers and lawn mowers competently. Five can actually plaster walls, not through receiving formal tuition, but because it was a natural development from filling holes in the walls with cement. Most can now tie shoelaces, they know when it's time for dinner or to go home, and they have learned how much to pay for chips in the local shop on Wednesdays, because they want to. Two of the older workers have asked for and are now receiving Adult Literacy lessons.*

This project is different from most. It was created by the people of Waunfawr and there is a distinct community involvement. To quantify or qualify the project's success or otherwise, readers would need to talk to people in the local Post Office, the chip shop, those living in the locality, and particularly those from the village who come into contact with the Antur workers from day to day in and around their homes. As well as the activities I have described the project workers help out in the local nursery school and the club for the elderly, and they act as caretakers of the local chapel because there was a need for that. They enjoy a natural interaction with local families.

I believe that if readers did make enquiries in every instance the response would be positive. The local people have seen individuals change from being meek and shy into confident adults; they have been amazed at their ability to handle intricate machinery; they are prepared to ask us to carry out work that needs to be done; they stop and talk on the road, or over the garden wall. They have said: 'Antur is part of the village now. If there was no money tomorrow we would ensure its survival'.[15]

Surely the real value of work is that it gives people a chance to be creative, in particular within the company of others, thus helping to develop valued relationships. Martin Ewing writes of the work done in the L'Arche communities: *Day provision in L'Arche focuses heavily on work, with an underlying belief that each person has the right to meaningful work which is accessible to them and in which they can become as autonomous as possible.*

By participating in creative work it is possible to instill in people a sense of their own value and worth. It is felt important that people have a choice in their work and that it can be adapted to meet individual needs as required. This therapeutic aspect of work is seen as being very important.

The priority of work in L'Arche, therefore, is people, their needs and gifts, rather than just productivity or profit. Although the work is strongly linked to an individual's growth, it must be seen as necessary and of value in itself. It is important, therefore, that products are sold on their merits and that people see they are making a valuable contribution to society.[16]

Unresolved issues about work include: the benefits trap which makes it difficult for people with learning difficulties to earn more than a token wage; the limited number of people who progress from work experience or part-time work to a full-time job; the lack of ongoing support for people in jobs. Nevertheless enough has been achieved to show what can be done.

By the end of the project I was convinced that work was one of the most promising routes to integration and, more importantly, gaining a sense of being valued and of realising one's worth. But there needs to be a variety of routes. To check what is appropriate the question to ask is, 'Will this enable this person to make and sustain relationships that enrich his or her life?'

Conclusion

This project's initial concern was to see how people with learning difficulties could be integrated better into the localities in which they lived. Then, through the process described in the first chapter, I saw that the fundamental need was for a full range of relationships. I have emphasised the importance of valuing existing and former friendships which may often be with others who have learning difficulties. The experience of the people I met in the project and the attitudes they had encountered to their friendships with other people with learning difficulties make that emphasis necessary.

The need for a full range of relationships, if properly understood, is synonymous with being a full part of society. Ultimately this will be brought about not by technicians who can create relationships for disabled people, but by citizens supporting fellow citizens – who happen to have learning difficulties – providing them with opportunities to choose and enjoy a range of fulfilling relationships. Of course, skills and resources will be needed and I have gone to considerable trouble to indicate what these are. Nevertheless, a fundamental shift in our approach to the enterprise is needed. As Deborah Gold says: *What must happen, instead, is a shift in the responsibility for relationship building back into the community, where it originated.*[17]

While we respect, honour and support the relationships that those with learning difficulties have with one another and, where necessary, help them re-establish relationships, this should not limit our efforts or their aspirations. Beyond is their continuing right to develop a full range of relationships with a full range of people, disabled or not. Encouraging the wider community to exercise its responsibilities does not imply that the services should withdraw and leave people and their families to get on as best they can. But the services must recognise that the way they offer that service must change.

I wrote over 20 years ago: *The simile of the interweaving of the informal helping and caring process active throughout society, and the contribution of the social services, is a sound one. It takes one beyond the stage of care in the community at home but living in isolation from those round about. It takes one beyond care in the community in institutions, even small ones, which have little involvement or share in the community. It takes one beyond care by the community, if by that one is suggesting that members of the community, untrained and unaided, should be left to get on with it. It takes one to the point where a partnership of the community at large and the social services is seen as essential by both. The caring done by families, friends, neighbours or larger, more organized groups of people is seen, recognized and acknowledged. An attempt is made to see both particular needs, and the strengths and limitations of the informal resources available. The social services seek to interweave their help so as to use and strengthen the help already given, make good the limitations and meet the needs. It is not a question of the social services plugging the gaps but rather of their working with society to enable society to close the gaps.*[18]

Sadly it needs saying as much as ever. It is a question of vision, something John McKnight catches in his article, Regenerating Community: *There appear to be three visions of society that dominate the discourse.*

The first is the therapeutic vision. This prospect sees the well-being of individuals as growing from an environment composed of professionals and their services. It envisions a world where there is a professional to meet every need, and the fee to secure each professional service is a right. This vision is epigrammatically expressed by those who see the ultimate liberty as 'the right to treatment'.

The second prospect is the advocacy vision. This approach foresees a world in which labelled people will be in an environment protected by advocates and advocacy groups. It conceives an individual whose world is guarded by legal advocates, support people, self-help groups, job developers, and housing locaters. Unlike the therapeutic vision, the advocacy approach conceives a defensive wall of helpers to protect an individual against an alien community. It seems to ensure a person's right to be a functioning individual.

The third approach is the community vision. It sees the goal as 'recommunalization' of exiled and labelled individuals. It understands the community as the basic context for enabling people to contribute their gifts. It sees community associations as contexts to create and locate jobs, provide opportunities for recreation and multiple friendships, and to become the political defender of the right of labelled people to be free from exile.

Those who seek to institute the community vision believe that beyond therapy and advocacy is the constellation of community association - the church, the bowling league, the garden club, the town paper, the Legion, the hardware store, and the township board. They see a society where those who were once labelled, treated, counselled, advised and protected are, instead, incorporated in a community where their contributions, capacities, gifts, and fallibilities will allow a network of relationships involving work, recreation, friendship, support, and the political power of being a citizen.[19]

I admitted in the first chapter that I found myself having to think ever more fundamentally. I believe John McKnight is right when he asks what sort of society we want. It is not a question of what sort of services we want for people with learning difficulties: it is a question of what sort of society we want for *ourselves*, a society in which people with learning difficulties are honoured and valued members.

John McKnight ends with what amounts to a statement of faith. If it sounds strange in our society then it is all the more important that it should be made:

It is only in community that we can be citizens. It is only in community that we can find care. It is only in community that we can hear people singing. And if you listen carefully, you can hear the words:

'I care for you because you are mine and I am yours' [20.]

References
1. Bayley, M., Seyd, R. and Tennant, A. (1989) Local Health and Welfare, A study of the Dinnington Project, Aldershot: Gower.
2. Brechin, A. and Swain, J. (1982) Aiding Human Functoning – Unit 7 of the Handicapped Person in the Community, Milton Keynes: Open University Press, pp.25, 26, and 26.
3. Glynn, M. and Hirst, M. (1992) This Year, Next Year, Sometime....? Learning Disability and Adulthood, London: National Development Team, p.71.
4. Kinsella, P. (1993) Supported Living: A new paradigm, Manchester: National Development Team.
5. Ibid. p.20.
6. Ibid. p.36.
7. Ibid. p.41.
8. Ibid. pp.16-17.
9. Ibid. p.19.
10. Mencap (1991) Empty Days... Empty Lives: A Mencap Report on day services - the vision and the reality, London: Mencap, p.10.
11. Booth, W. and Fielden, S. (1992) Second Opinions: Students' Views of Swallow Street Centre, p.12.
12. Connolly, J. (1993) Real Life, Soundtrack, (published by National Development Team) Issue 10, October 1993, p.11.
13. Wertheimer, Alison (1992) Changing Lives: Supported Employment and People with Learning Disabilities, Manchester: National Development Team, p.32.
14. Lister, T., Ellis, L., Phillips, T., O'Bryan, A., Beyer, S. and Kilsby, M. (1992) Survey of Supported Employment Services in England, Scotland and Wales, Manchester: National Development Team, p.40.
15. Evans, H.V. (1987) Antur Waunfawr: Its early development and achievements, *Mental Handicap*, Vol.15, September 1987, pp.108-111.
16. Ewing, M. (1993) Self-Sufficiency, *Inside*, supplement of *Community Care*, 25 Nov 1993, p.3.
17. Gold, D. (1980) A look beyond Leisure Buddy Programs, The Pursuit of Leisure: Enriching the Lives of People who have a Disability, Ontario, Canada: G. Allan Roeher Institute, p.48.
18. Bayley, M. (1973) Mental Handicap and Community Care, London: Routledge and Kegan Paul, p.343.
19. McKnight, J. (1989) Regenerating Community, The Pursuit of Leisure: Enriching the Lives of People who have a Disability, Ontario, Canada: G. Allan Roeher Insitute, p.27.
20. Ibid. p.30.

Appendices

A. Friendship schemes

To my knowledge, the most fully worked-out and systematic programme for setting up a scheme is: The One-to-One Resource Pack: a guide to establishing and running local schemes through which people with learning difficulties can gain new friendships in their communities (1990). Available from One-to-One, 404 Camden Road, London N7 0SJ (0171-700-5574).

Another systematic 'how-to-do-it' book comes from Jodie Walsh: Lets Make Friends (1986), in the Human Horizon series from Souvenir Press, London. Roy McConkey's Who Cares? Community Involvement with Handicapped People (1987), is from the same series but gives a rather wider context.

Jeannie Sutcliffe's Integration for Adults with Learning Difficulties, (1992), National Institute of Adult Continuing Education (NIACE), has a number of helpful examples of adult education schemes and is good at saying what went well and what the problems were. It follows on from her book, mentioned in the main text, Adults with Learning Difficultes, Education for Choice and Empowerment (1990), NIACE/Open University Press.

Communitas (PO Box 374, Manchester CT 06040, USA) develops strategies which enable people with learning disabilities to integrate with the community and to gain a full range of friends and acquaintances. Relevant publications:

>Beth Mount, Pat Beeman and George Ducharme, What Are We Learning About Bridge-building? (1988). Summary of a dialogue between people seeking to build community for people with disabilities.
>One Candle Power: building bridges into community life for people with disabilities (1989).
>Person-centered Development: a journey in learning to listen to people with disabilities (1991).

In a similar vein, Mary O'Connell's The Gift of Hospitality: opening the doors of community life to people with disabilities (1988). Center for Urban Studies and Policy Research, Northwestern University and Department of Rehabilitation Services, Illinois.

The G. Allan Roeher Institute in Ontario (Canada's National Institute for the Study of Public Policy Affecting Persons with an Intellectual Impairment) publishes much good writing about people with learning disabilities and on this particular theme: Making Friends: developing relationships between people with a disability and other members of the community (1990), and The Pursuit of Leisure: enriching the lives of people who have a disability (1989). The latter has an excellent chapter by Deborah Gold (quoted in Chapter X) called, A Look Beyond Leisure Building Programmes, which talks about the positive advantages of such programmes: *...people with a handicap get the chance to meet and even to know typical citizens when otherwise they might not get that chance. Second, the volunteer could become a friend, although whether this happens or not is not usually due to the program itself. People with handicaps also get chances to try new things and to be involved in the community, even if these opportunities are somewhat limited. Thus, lives may be enriched. Also, typical citizens receive the opportunity to get to know someone with a handicap on a more intimate basis than if they were spending time in a program setting. The opportunity may be there for advocates to emerge from some of these relationships. Public education may take place as people are seen to value each other in public places. Finally, it is possible that, through these sorts of relationships, others may develop and people's networks could expand* (p46).

But points to some important limitations: *What people are really in need of are friends: people they can count on in a crisis; people who feel they benefit from the relationship; people who like them for who they are. What people with handicaps often get in this kind of model is a volunteer – someone who is almost always the giver while the handicapped person is viewed as the taker, the one 'for' whom things are done.*

The relationship itself in these programs is unnatural. People are matched together who previously were complete strangers. Like Big Brothers and Big Sisters, there is little thought given in these programs to the strengthening of existing relationships in people's lives. Thus, professionals take control over what should be a very natural, or at least facilitated, process. This problem of 'artificiality' is augmented by the fact that the volunteer often has to be a specialist of some sort, as shown by the amount of training he or she often receives. There is a direct contradiction between this concept and that of friendship. The latter usually more often begins because of a spark or magic between two people, having things in common, or simply liking each other. It develops with support from both parties, and from outsiders, like parents and other friends (pp44-45).

It concludes:
...we are called upon to understand the difference between companionship and friendship. Whether a companionship becomes a deeper friendship probably depends more on the individuals involved than anything else. A program can't offer what a friendship does. We feel responsible to create programs in which people can have friends. If we are not careful, soon we will have 'friendship technicians' and we will be able to study this topic at college or university.

What must happen, instead, is a shift in the responsibility for relationship-building back into the community, where it originated. Certainly, some 'Leisure Buddy' programs can be the starting places for this to occur. But it can happen elsewhere as well. Parents, service providers, and volunteers can all have an influence in facilitating friendships between persons with handicaps and other citizens in the community. 'Friendship' programs must rethink how they operate and let go of people. We must give up control of people's lives if we want connections to happen. With support, leisure can occur out of individual needs and personal interests rather than structured programs and arranged relationships (pp47-48).

Finally, for a marvellous book about a man with learning difficulties and a great gift for friendship, read Therese Vanier's Nick, Man of the Heart, (1993), Dublin, Gill & Macmillan.

Appendix B. Use of the matrix

I have chosen two strongly contrasting examples (opposite page). John and Philippa Mason were very well integrated. They needed quite a lot of help and they received it from his brother, who called in almost every day, and his sister and husband who came once a week to do the laundry. John and Philippa were retired but had both attended training centres. They occasionally went to the hostel where they had met to see two members of staff in particular. Hostel staff had helped them arrange their wedding and the reception was held on the premises. They continued to attend regularly the church where they were married. However, the richness of their relationships depended on receiving practical help – the 'appropriate aids for living' discussed in Chapter X. The major part of this came from John's brother and sister but back-up from the social worker, the Oldale Support Group and the hostel staff had been critical at some stages.

By contrast, the poverty of Christopher Johnson's relationships is all too clear. His almost total reliance on his elderly mother is obvious and she receives little support except from Christopher's brother and sister-in-law.

The matrix makes the richness of John Mason's position and the poverty and precariousness of Christopher Johnson's easy to see. It also indicates where action needs to be taken.

John Mason

Basic Human Emotional and Cognitive Needs

Structural Factors, ie. Settings or Occasions	Belonging and Attachment	Social Integration	Nurturance	Reassurance of worth	Exercise of Choice	Reliable Assistance	Guidance from respected others
Home/ Residence	Wife	Many local acquaintances	Wife	Wife	Control of flat with wife		
Work/ Education/ Occupation		Helping in local newspaper shop on Saturdays			Going shopping		
Leisure/ Social/ Spiritual		Local Church Luncheon Club	Circle of friends, esp. looking after Harry Grey	Church circle of friends	Choosing friends	Church Oldale Support Group	Vicar
Supportive Services and People	Brother and sister					Brother and sister Oldale Support Group	Brother and sister Social worker Staff of nearby hostel (where the couple met)

Christopher Johnson

Basic Human Emotional and Cognitive Needs

Structural Factors, ie. Settings or Occasions	Belonging and Attachment	Social Integration	Nurturance	Reassurance of worth	Exercise of Choice	Reliable Assistance	Guidance from respected others
Home/ Residence	Mother			Mother		Mother	Mother
Work/ Education/ Occupation				Formerly Mary Cartwright Friend at ATC		Formerly ATC	Formerly key worker at ATC
Leisure/ Social/ Spiritual							
Supportive Services and People	? brother and sister-in-law						

Appendix C. Thumbnail sketches of people mentioned

1. Peter Akers. 'Bit of a loner'. Turned his back on you. p35, p47
2. Brian Attwell. Lived in small group home. Attended training centre. Unhappy at loss of industrial contract work. Friend of Anthony Turner. p36, pp38-39 ,p42, p57
3. Josie Banner. Very disabled person living contentedly with her parents. pp45-46
4. Sharon Barker. Over dependence on aide leading to relationship breaking down. p77.
5. Kate Briggs. Able woman living in hostel which she hated, for whom Circle of Support was formed. p59, p79
6. Philip Brindley. Lived in health authorityl house with Jason Havering. Cheerful character who attended local Anglican Church. p11, pp57-59,pp71-72
7. Tom Bristow. Member of Helden Club. Mother died. Friend of Edward and Cliff Jacques. p64
8. Felicity Broadhurst. Had moved to own flat with help of parents. Friend of Hilary Fenton. Member of Victor Gentle group. p36, pp55-56
9. Mrs Carter. Volunteer who took Jason Havering to the Roman Catholic Church. p74
10. Mary Cartwright. Friend of Christopher Johnson, whom she sees no longer. pp25-26
11. John Edwards. Used to live in hostel. Now in flat by himself. Friend of Henry Potts. pp37-38
12. Harry Evans. Volunteer who worked with Arnold Trapman.p48
13. Matthew Exton. Quite disabled man who lived on his own with support from home aides after his mother died. pp52-54
14. Hilary Fenton. Had moved into her own flat with help of her parents. Friend of Felicity Broadhurst and member of Victor Gentle's group. p36, pp55-56
15. Martin and Jenny Fry. Married after tempestuous early history. Had home aide five days a week. He was keen on snooker. pp60-61
16. Victor Gentle. 'Volunteer' who supported an imaginative informal group of friends. pp55
17. Jack Grant. Older man who shared a house with Harry Vaynol for 15 years. Geoff Price also lived with them. pp61-62
18. Stephen Hardwick. Deaf man who went to his local pub regularly. pp69
19. Mark Hastings. Lived with widowed mother. Lacked adequate sense of 'belonging and attachment'. Unsuccessful link with rambling club. pp20-22
20. June Haston. Used same training centre as Michael Preston with

whom she was friendly. pp39-41

21. Jason Havering. Lived in health authority house with Philip Brindley. Attended local Roman Catholic church. p11, pp57-59

22. Hilda and Frank Hessing. Friends of Bruce Mander, who looked after Hilda when Frank went into hospital. p64

23. Jane Hodson. Lived with elderly parents, and wanted boyfriends like everyone else. p51

24. Edward and Cliff Jacques. Members of the Helden Club. Friends of Tom Bristow. p 64

25. Christopher Johnson. Severely disabled. Lived with widowed mother. Inadequate structure for building new relationships. pp25-26, p46

26. Dennis Jones. Lived in small group home. Proud of his job in industrial unit which recycled paper. pp35-36

27. John and Philippa Mason. Married couple living in Hillside area. Centre of a small network of friends. p64

28. Hugh Milson. Went via a special adult education class to an integrated one. p83

29. Jennifer Morton. Young woman living with her parents, with a good range of relationships. pp46-47

30. Arthur Needles. Lived with parents. Very unsure of himself. Good link with Jennifer Parsons, retired teacher. p22

31. Freda and Geoffrey Parker. Met at training centre and subsequently married. p41, pp56-57, pp91-92

32. Jack and Eileen Parsons. Obsessive relationship. Jack lacked the weaker ties of ordinary friendship. p23

33. James Pearson. Quite able man. Attended training centre. Linked up with volunteer, John Hilton, to play snooker at local club. p48

34. Garry Phillips. Had lost first mother, then aunt. Sometimes was cross-dressing. p54

35. Miss Polkington. Volunteer working with Philip Brindley. p58

36. Henry Potts. Lived in staffed residence. Friend of John Edwards. pp37-38

37. Michael Preston. Quiet man living with widowed mother. Friend of June Haston. p39-41

38. Geoff Price. Worked as a contract gardener, very satisfactory pattern of life. pp44

39. Margaret Race. Lived with parents, who were Catholics. Possibility of link with Catholic family explored. p50

40. Jane Raffles. Deaf volunteer working with Philip Brindley. p58

41. Stan Rivers. Apparently well integrated, but profoundly unhappy. pp1-3

42. Pamela Scribbens. Lived with loving professional parents, but few incentives to develop own relationships. p49

43. Desmond Slater. Banned from training centre and had to be looked after by his elderly grandmother. p84

44. Arnold Trapman. Young man living with parents. Obsessive behaviour. Good relationship formed with volunteer of his own age, Harry Evans. p48

45. Andrew Trend. Volunteer working with Philip Brindley. p58

46. Douglas Trinder. Attended training centre. Limited social skills and loud voice. p35, p48

47. Anthony Turner. Lived in tower block. Over retirement age. Friend of Brian Attwell. pp38-39, p42, p59

48. Harry Vaynol. Older man who had shared a house with Jack Grant for 15 years. Geoff Price also lived with them. pp61-62

49. Mavis and Simon West. Met at hostel and married. Mavis had problems coping with drugs for her epilepsy in the past. p41

50. Bernard Wiles. Had to negotiate a suitable arrangement with the church he attended. p85

51. Glen Williams. Able young man who did not want to make friends with people at the training centre he attended. Became pen friends with children he met at camping sites. p51

Appendix D. The context of the project
Resources available
With only half of me available, close collaboration with other workers, people and organisations in the area was necessary. It also ensured I was not missed when the project finished.

The area
The area is almost entirely residential with housing varying widely in type and quality. It is roughly one and a half miles square and slopes down, sometimes quite steeply, to a major road, which is a clear boundary. At the lower end the architecture is mostly late nineteenth or early twentieth century and houses vary from artisanal to quite substantial buildings, some in multiple occupation. Much of the housing is terraced. Further up, on one side, is a large inter-war council housing estate, only a small part of which was included in the project area. In the middle, is another council estate built in the early 1960s, with inter-war private housing on the other side. At the top is a belt of owner-occupied housing, mostly post-war.

The 1991 Census gives the population as about 28,000, with just over 4 per cent recorded as non-white. In the polling district with the largest non-white population the proportion was just over 11 per cent. Unemployment was highest on the inter-war council housing estate (28 per cent), and lowest in the middle-class owner-occupied part (5.8 per cent). In four of the 14 polling districts making up the area the unemployment was over 20 per cent. Pensioners totalled just over 20 per cent.

Although the lower part, on the main road, is not far from the town centre, there are two quite large shopping areas. One, Oldale, includes a library, a community centre, a local authority housing office, a doctor's surgery and a health centre, besides a good array of shops, two pubs and a church. About a mile down the road is a slightly smaller shopping centre with two doctors' surgeries, one linked closely with a community centre (next door) in which a local health project operates. This practice has a strong community orientation. Nearby is also an old school now open for community use and host to a variety of classes and activities. There is also a commercial snooker hall. One of five churches in the area is on the edge of the shopping centre and runs an active programme with sessions for both young and elderly people. A third community hall nearby has a lunch club run by one of the receptionists at the general practice with strong community links. This older part has a more cohesive feel to it than that further up the hillside. There is one residents association here; another, has its base in the Oldale Community Centre in the larger shopping centre up the hill.

Statutory and other resources
There is no social services office but there are two hostels for people with learning difficulties and a small locally based day centre. This has developed a number of links with organisations in the locality. In addition, two social workers run a support group for people with learning difficulties in the Oldale Community Centre. Two community nurses work with people with learning disabilities in the area.

Mencap has a centre just out of the area attended by many people with learning difficulties living in the area. This has a wide range of daytime, evening and week-end activities, including a swimming club and a hiking club. There is also a small private group home for six people.

Overall the services must be described as *in* the area rather than *of* the area. The lack of a local base for either social workers or community nurses meant there was little in-depth understanding of the area. The locally based day centre was a partial exception, and the community-oriented general practice another.